PRONUNCIATION CARD GAMES

Linnea Henry

with illustrations by

Dorothy Henry

PRO LINGUA  ASSOCIATES

Pro Lingua Associates, Publishers
P.O. Box 1348
Brattleboro, Vermont 05302 USA
Office: 802 257 7779
Orders: 800 366 4775
E-mail: Orders@ProLinguaAssociates.com
Webstore: www.ProLinguaAssociates.com
SAN: 216-0579

At Pro Lingua
our objective is to foster an approach
to learning and teaching that we call
interplay, *the* **inter***action of language*
learners and teachers with their materials,
with the language and culture,
and with each other in active, creative
and productive **play**.

The original concept of using index cards for pronunciation games, and eight of the games were created by Linnea Henry. The games Sort 'n' Stack, Stress Match and Say it Again were contributed by Ray Clark.

This book was set in Century Schoolbook type. It was printed and bound by Walch Printing in Portland, Maine. It was designed by Arthur A. Burrows.

The illustrations for sets #1-13 and set # 16 are by Dorothy Henry. The drawings of the Presidents and maps of states and provinces are from the *Art Explosion 250,000 Images* collection © 1997 by Nova Development Corporation.

Printed in the United States of America.
Third Printing 2011. 3700 copies.

Acknowledgments

I'd like to thank all of the students who have inspired and taught me, especially Jesús, Alejandra, Sylvia, Johan, Young-Hee, Hyun-Soo, Monica, Ridvan, Min-Seok, Fabian, and Daniella. Special thanks to Mike Micciula for his help with the final manuscript.

LH

And thanks to my students in the Master of Arts in Teaching Program at the School for International Training for their comments on my card games featuring suprasegmentals.

RCC

Dedicated
to the memory of my father,
Clemence Henry.

LH

Contents

Consonants

Syllables and Stress

PRONUNCIATION
CARD
GAMES

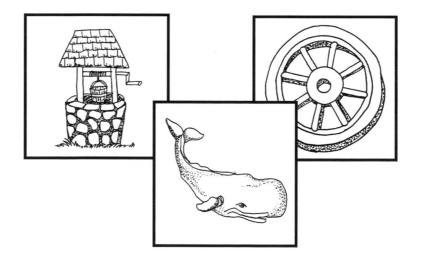

Editor's Pronouncement on Pronouns

We at Pro Lingua Associates are offering a solution to the vexing "he/she" pronoun problem. We have come to the conclusion that when a reference is made to a grammatically singular third person, and that person is indefinite (and hence gender is unknown or unimportant), we will use the third person plural forms, *they,them,their(s)*. We are fully aware that historically these forms represent grammatical plurality. However, there are clear instances in the English language where the third person plural form is used to refer to a preceding indefinite, grammatically singular pronoun. Examples:

> Everyone says this, don't **they**?
> Nobody agrees with us, but we will ignore **them**.

If you will accept the examples above, it is not a major step to find the following acceptable:

> The learner of English should find this easier because **they** can avoid the confusion of *he* or *she*, the awkwardness of *he or she*, and the implicit sexism of using *he* for everybody.

So in this book, you will find instructions to the student such as, *Once **a player** collects all four cards in a suit, **they** put them in a pile, face down.* This is our solution to an uncomfortable problem. We encourage you to try it out, and we invite your comments.

RCC for PLA

Introduction

What are pronunciation card games? Pronunciation card games are an enjoyable and effective resource for ESL teachers to use in teaching pronunciation. The instructions for eleven different games follow this introduction, and the cards for playing the games are easily made by copying the included sheets of originals. Although the pages can be cut from the book, it is recommended that the book be kept intact as the original source for making sets of cards.

How are pronunciation card games organized? There are two main types of cards, segmental and suprasegmental cards.

Sets 1-12 are for practicing individual sounds (segmentals). Each set contains a collection of pictures, (each picture is called a suit) representing different words. These words all contain potentially confusing pairs of sounds (minimal pairs). A minimal pair of words contains only one segmental difference. For example, Set # 1 represents the /iy/ – /i/ contrast and includes six basic pairs: *sheep-ship, heels-hills, meat-mitt, peels-pills, beans-bins,* and *wheel-will.* The games can be played with these six basic pairs, but to allow for a greater variety of games, two "extra" pairs are appended to each set. Therefore, if the game is played a second time, the extra pairs can be substituted to provide some variety. In Set # 1, the extra cards are *leap-lip* and *cheek-chick.* By playing the segmental practice card games, students will first learn to hear the difference between the two contrasting sounds in each pair and then develop the ability to recognize and produce the individual sounds.

Sets 13-16 are used for practicing stress, a suprasegmental aspect of pronunciation. (See the appendix for additional information about stress.) In these games, the students are challenged to hear and produce three levels of word stress – primary, secondary, and weak – as well as major stress in a phrase or sentence. For example, *Washington* is pronounced with heavy stress on the first syllable, *Wash.* The other syllables, *ing* and *ton,* have weaker stress. The second syllable, *ing,* does have some stress, and the vowel is not completely reduced The students can learn to distinguish and produce the three word stress levels They will also be able to hear and use contrastive stress, *a BIG heart in a square* (not a small heart), and sentence and contrastive-emphatic stress: *Aunt Abigail drove HOME. Didn't she WALK home?   No, she DROVE home.*

How do I make my card games? To create your own sets of cards, it is recommended that you copy the relevant pages, cut out the cards, and glue them to index cards so that the students can't see through the cards, and so that the cards can be used over and over. The cards will last even longer if they are laminated. If you make more than one copy of the same set, use index cards of a different color for each copy or put a number on the back of each separate copy.

What makes pronunciation card games effective?

• **Discovery.** By playing the games, students have the opportunity to experiment and explore the pronunciation of similar sounds. Students can then discover their own best ways to distinguish between the sounds, in addition to the tactics suggested by their teacher and peers.

• **Repetition.** The games provide for considerable repetition, but in the context of an engaging game, rather than in a mechanical repetition drill. Students have fun as they repeat and listen to the problem sounds over and over, without feeling that they are doing a boring or blindly repetitive exercise.

• **Adaptability.** The segmental games can be played by students at any level, from beginning to advanced, while the suprasegmental games are better suited to intermediate and advanced level students. The games are enjoyable for students of any age.

• **Feedback.** There is immediate and ongoing feedback from other students. When a breakdown in communication occurs, the students work together to repair it.

• **Accuracy through Peer Correction.** Although the teacher may still work on accuracy by providing corrections, students will generally decide by themselves from peer feedback whether their pronunciation is comprehensible.

• **Pronunciation vs. Spelling.** Pronunciation is practiced without the interference of spelling. Since students are working with pictures rather than written words, they can focus on the sounds of the words without the distraction of spelling.

2

• **Context.** Individual sounds are practiced in the context of sentences. Unlike rote repetition drills, each sound is practiced within a sentence, as it would be spoken in conversation.

• **Physical response.** The sounds are practiced in a meaningful context, because there is a physical, material response to each play in the game, and there is a purpose for each play.

• **Group consensus.** This is perhaps the aspect that sets Pronunciation Card Games apart the most from other activities designed to teach pronunciation. Teaching English pronunciation is a complex task, especially since pronunciation varies from region to region and country to country. When introducing Pronunciation Card Games, the teacher may model one variety of English pronunciation and the students will naturally try to imitate this model. However, because of the nature of the games, it is also possible for the students to work together as a community to determine a mutually intelligible pronunciation of each sound. Having learned the process of developing intelligible pronunciation from group consensus, students will be better equipped to communicate effectively in the larger, global English-speaking community.

• **Pronunciation Card Games are fun!**

General Instructions

Before class:

Choose the game and the set of cards the students will be working with and the particular pictures they will use in the game. Then make copies according to the instructions for the game. Next, you will need to paste the pictures on cards.

In class:

Before playing the card games, make sure that the students are familiar and comfortable with the vocabulary represented on the cards. Warm-ups (see the next section) are particularly important prior to playing any of the Pronunciation Card Games. Whatever warm-up you choose to use, it should serve two purposes:

- To introduce students to the vocabulary and the pictures used to represent it.
- To introduce students to the sound contrasts or the suprasegmental features to be practiced.

The type of warm-up that you do will vary according to the level of your students, your students' learning styles, and your own approach to teaching.

Suggested Warm-Ups

for Sets 1-12

Show the students a card from each pair, and have them guess the word it represents. The second card in each pair will be easier to guess, for obvious reasons! If the students don't guess the word, the teacher can give the students a hint or supply the name. For example:

> Teacher (holding up *sheep*): *What's the name of this card?*
> Student 1: *A lamb?*
> T: *It could be a lamb, but it has another name.*
> S2: *A sheep?*
> T: *That's right!* (holding up *ship*) What's this?
> S3: *A boat?*
> T: *Well, it could be a boat, but it sounds more like* sheep.
> S4: *Is it a ship?*

After all of the suits (pictures) are named, the teacher holds the cards up at random, and the students call out the names of the suits. Then continue until they are familiar with the names of all of the suits.

The teacher distributes the cards among the students. The teacher calls out, *Show me some peels.* The students hold up the cards illustrating *peels*. If some students hold up the wrong card, the teacher corrects: *Did I say* peels *or* pills?

The students are divided into groups of four. The cards are redistributed so that each group has four each of four different suits, representing two minimal pairs. For example, one group may have *beans-bins* and *wheel-will*. Another group may have *heels-hills* and *sheep-ship*. The students then take turns asking each other, *Show me a* wheel, or *Show me a* will. If there is disagreement, the students may try to clarify their pronunciation among themselves, or they may ask the teacher for help.

When the students have developed a familiarity with the sounds in question, they are ready to play the game. It is not necessary for them to have the sounds perfectly under control, because by playing the game, their ability to produce and hear the sounds will become better. As they play, they will ask each other clarification questions, such as, *Did you say* heels *or* hills? and they will probably break into laughter on their way to clearer pronunciation.

Suggested Warm-Ups for Sets 13-16

Set 13

This is a relatively simple set to introduce. The vocabulary is limited to *heart, circle, square, big, small, in,* and *near*. Nevertheless, it might be necessary to show the different cards and ask the students to identify the vocabulary items above. For example:

> Teacher (holding up a card): *What's in the square?*
> Student 1: *A heart.*
> T: *Is it a big heart or a small heart?*
> S 2: *It's a small heart.*
> etc.

The main point of this game, however, is placing the stress on the variable that is being contrasted. Therefore, it would be useful for the teacher to demonstrate and exaggerate the stress pattern in the sentence.

> Teacher: *Is this a BIG heart or a SMALL heart ?*
> S 1: *It's big heart.*
> T: *That's right, it's a BIG heart. Is it in a circle? No! It's in a SQUARE. Where is it ?*
> SS: *In a SQUARE!*

Set 14

The names of states and provinces are used to practice identification of syllables and the syllable that has the primary stress. A map of the U.S. and Canada would be useful for introducing the names of the states and provinces. The simplest warm-up would be to have the students hear and repeat the place names that would be used in the sort 'n' stack game. Give each student a blank map of the U.S. and Canada, and have them label it with the state and province names as you point them out on a large wall map or on an overhead. Note that only 18 place names are included as cards in this book, but it would be very simple to make your own cards from the lists of additional states and provinces in Appendix D. Of course, each time you introduce a new list you should be sure the students have a chance to say and repeat the names.

Set 15

This set uses the names of Presidents of the U.S. to practice the placement of major and minor stress in names. The two sets included in this book contain the names of the presidents that the students might know or recognize. Nevertheless, it would be a good idea to make an overhead of the President cards (but not the stress cards) and have the students repeat the names of the Presidents before playing the game.

Set 16

This set features four characters, four means of transportation, four places, and four time expressions. The cards themselves don't have the words, and so it would be necessary to go through the cards once or twice to familiarize the students with the names and phrases that the cards represent. For example, after showing and naming the four character cards (an overhead would be useful here), the teacher might carry out a short question-answer practice:

Teacher: *Who's this* (showing or pointing to a card)?
Students: *It's Aunt Abigail.*
T: *Are you sure? Isn't it Polly Pigtails?*
SS: *No. It's Aunt Abigail.*
T: *And who are they?*
SS: *The Bruise Brothers.*
T: *Aren't they the BLUES Brothers?*
SS: *No! They are the BRUISE Brothers.*
T: *Where are they going* (showing the office card)?
SS: *To the office.*

Sort 'n' Stack

Players: 3-4 in each group.

Sets: Selected cards from various sets, except sets 13 (Hearts), 15 (Stress-Match), and 16 (Say It Again). For vowels and consonants choose three sounds that are somewhat similar, for example, iy - i - e. See the recommendations below.

Cards: Each group gets 18 cards. Normally, each group is working on the same three sounds. This means that if you have three groups, you need to have three copies of each card. However, it is also possible to have the groups working on different sounds and then switch cards after each game so that each group works with each group of sounds. For example:

Group #1
uses iy - i - e

Group # 2
uses e - æ - a

Group # 3
uses æ - a - ə

Recommended games:

iy - i - e	b - v - f	ch - sh - j
e - æ - a	p - f - b	th - s - t
ae - a - ə	s - z - sh	*th* - d - t

Objective: To sort a group of cards into three stacks, each stack having the same vowel or consonant sound, for example, sh<u>ee</u>p, p<u>ee</u>ls, m<u>ea</u>t, etc. For the game using set #14 (States and Provinces), the objective is to sort the cards into stacks that have the same number of syllables (Syllable Sort 'n' Stack) or stress on the same syllable (Stress Sort 'n' Stack). See pages 18 and 19.

Play: A well-shuffled set of 18 different cards is placed face down in front of each group. At the sound of "Go" each group picks up the top card and places it face up on the table. From this point on, as each card is turned over, the group decides which stack it belongs in, according to the pronunciation of the key sound in the word. When the group has sorted all 18 cards into three stacks, they signal the teacher that they're finished.

Win: In the competitive version, the first group to finish calls out "Finished!" and play stops. They read their solution, and if they're correct the group is declared the winner.

In the non-competitive version, each group completes its stacking, and then the first group to finish reads/says the words in their stacks. The other groups listen, and challenge if they want to.

Special Note for Using Set #15 (States and Provinces). There are two games that can be played with these cards. In game #1 (very easy) the students sort the cards into three stacks according to the number of syllables (2, 3, 4) in the word. In Game #2 the students sort the cards according to which syllable has the primary (heaviest) stress - 1st, 2nd, 3rd, 4th, etc. A list of additional states and provinces is in Appendix D and a list of cities is in Appendix E.

Four of a Kind

Players: Four in each group. If groups of four aren't possible, there can be one of six. If there's a group of five, two students can share a hand as one player.

Sets: Choose one set from among sets 1-12.

Cards: For each group of four, you should have 16 cards. The group should have four copies of each pair, for example, four sheep, four ships, four peels, four pills. If you make four copies of the entire set (a total of 48 cards), you could have four groups playing at the same time. After they complete one game, they exchange cards with another group. Example:

Group 1
sheep, ship
peels, pills

Group 2
hills, heels
beans, bins

Group 3
meat, mitt
wheel, will

Group 4
leap, lip
cheek, chick

Deal: Four cards to each player.

Objective: Collect four cards in the same suit.

Play: The person to the dealer's left asks any other player, by name, for a particular card. The person asking must already have at least one card of that suit. For example, if Carlos has two ships, a sheep and a will, he may ask Mariko, "Do you have a ship?" If Mariko has the ship, she must give it to Carlos. If Mariko has two ships, she gives only one. Carlos then gives Mariko any card he doesn't want, being careful that no other player sees the card. The play continues this way until Carlos asks another player for a card that player doesn't have. His turn is then over, and the player to his left asks another player for a particular card. The play continues until someone collects all four cards of a suit. That person calls out the name of the suit and lays down the cards.

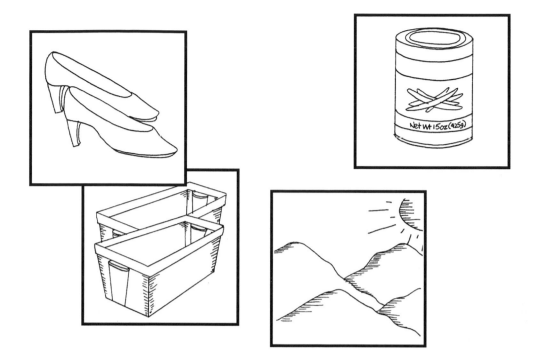

Win: The first player to collect four cards in the same suit wins.

Asking for clarification: If a player asks another player for a card and the player who was asked can't understand clearly, they should ask for clarification:

> Carlos: *Do you have any heels?*
> Mariko: *Did you say* hills *or* heels?
> Carlos: Heels. *Do you have any heels?*

If, on the other hand, a player misunderstands and delivers the wrong card, the person receiving the card corrects the mistake:

> Student: *No, these are bins. I asked for beans. Do you have any beans?*

Asking for clarification is an important part of the game. It's a good opportunity to explore the subtleties of pronunciation.

Bingo

Players: Players may work with a partner or individually.

Sets: One set from among sets 1-12.

Cards: Two copies of a set for each player (each player or team should have 24 cards) and an extra two copies for the caller.

Objective: Turn over five cards in a row.

Play: One of the students (or the teacher) is the caller. The other players lay their cards out face up in a five by five grid, with an empty space in the middle. Players may place a wild card or other object in the middle. The caller shuffles their cards and draws one card at a time, calling out the name of the card. The players look for the same card, and if they have it, they turn it over. When a player or team has turned over a complete row (vertical, horizontal, or diagonal), they shout "Bingo!" and receive one point. Each player may take one turn as a caller.

Win: The player with the most points after everyone has called once wins.

Variation: To develop listening discrimination, the teacher may be the caller throughout the game, instead of the students.

Go Fish

Players: Two to four in each group.

Sets: Choose one set of six pairs from among sets 1-12.

Cards: One set of 12 cards for each player plus two extra suits.

Deal: Four cards for each player; the rest go in the fish pile.

Objective: Get rid of all your cards.

Play: The person to the left of the dealer asks any player, by name, for a particular card. The person asking must already possess a card in that suit. If the person who is asked for that card has it, they must give it to the person who asked for it. In this case, the person asking may again ask any player for another card. The play continues until a player doesn't have a requested card. That player then tells the person who is asking, "Go fish!" and the asker must take a card from the top of the fish pile. The player who didn't have the requested card may now ask any player for a particular card, provided they have one in that suit. Once a player collects all four cards in one suit, they put them in a pile face down.

Win: The first player to have no cards in their hand wins.

Pronunciation Poker

Players: Four in each group.

Cards: Four copies of a set, plus four wild cards. (Wild cards may be taken from any other set not in use.)

Deal: Twelve cards for each player; the remaining four go face down in the middle.

Objective: Be the first to collect three sets of four, or twelve different cards.

Play: The person to the left of the dealer offers to exchange one specific card for another specific card. For example, "I'll trade a wheel for a ship." The first player to say, "I accept," trades the specified card, and it becomes that player's turn. If no one accepts, the person asking places a card face up in the center and takes a card from the face down pile. This person can now make another offer. Whoever accepts the offer takes the turn and makes the next offer. When a player can lay down three sets of four, or twelve different cards, the play is over.

When the play is over, players receive the following points:

3 sets of 4	3 points
12 different cards	3 points
2 sets of 4	2 points
1 set of 4	1 point

Win: The first player to reach 11 points wins.

Dominoes

Players: Two to four.

Cards: Set 13; two complete sets per player.

Deal: Eight cards to each player, the rest in a pile.

Objective: Be the first player to get rid of all your cards.

Play: The dealer places the first card from the pile face up in the middle of the table, and states the name of the card. The name of the card describes the heart in terms of three variables: size (big or small), place (in or near), and shape (circle or square). For example: "It's a big heart near a circle." The person to the left of the dealer lays a card next to the first card. This card must have two variables in common with the first card, and one different. The player says the name of the card, emphasizing the difference. For example: "It's a big heart IN a circle." In this case, size and shape are the same, but place is different. The next player lays down a card in which two variables are the same as the last card, and one is different, again emphasizing the difference. For example: "It's a SMALL heart in a circle." The game could progress as follows:

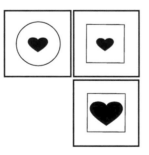

1. It's a small heart in a circle.
2. It's a small heart in a SQUARE.
3. It's a BIG heart in a square.
4. It's a big heart in a CIRCLE.
5. It's a big heart NEAR a circle.

If a player doesn't have a card that can be played, that is, a card in which only one variable changes, they must draw a card from the pile. If this card can be played, they must play it. If not, they continue to draw until they find one they can play.

When there are no cards left in the pile, any player who doesn't have a card that they can play says, "Pass," and the play passes to the next player.

Win: The first player to use all their cards wins.

Liar

Players: Four to eight in each group.

Cards: Four to eight copies of set 13.

Deal: All cards except one; the last card goes face up in the middle of the table. Some players may have extra cards.

Objective: Be the first player to use all your cards.

Play: The dealer calls out the name (size-place-shape) of the card lying face up on the table, for example: "It's a big heart in a circle." The person to the left of the dealer must lay a card face down on top of the first card, calling out its name. This card must have two variables in common with the first card, and one different, for example: "It's a big heart NEAR a circle." In this case, size and shape are the same, but place is different. The player should emphasize the word *near*. The next player must lay a card face down in which two variables are the same as the last card, and one is different, for example: "It's a small heart near a circle." The game could progress as follows:

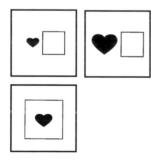

Dealer: It's a big heart near a square.
S1: It's a SMALL heart near a square.
S2: It's a small heart IN a square.
S3: It's a small heart in a CIRCLE.
S4: It's a BIG heart in a circle.
Dealer: It's a SMALL heart in a circle.

If a player doesn't have a card they can play, that is, a card in which only one variable changes, they must lie. So in the above example, the next player could play any card they have in their hand, and call it, for example, a small heart in a square.

If one player (A) suspects another player (B) of lying, A can call B a liar and turn over the last card to check. If player B has lied, A takes all the cards in the stack. If B was telling the truth, B takes the stack. Whoever takes the stack chooses a card to lay face up on the table, and the play continues with the player sitting to their right.

Win: The first player to play their last card and either be telling the truth if challenged, or have the next player cover their card without being challenged, wins.

Optional rule: If a player notices that another player has named a card with two differences, instead of just one, they can point out the mistake and the first player must take the pile of cards.

Syllable Sort 'n' Stack

Players: 3-4 in each group.

Set: 14a or 14b

Cards: Each group gets 18 cards — one full set.

Objective: To sort a group of cards into three stacks, each stack having the same number of syllables. For the game using set 14a, there are six each of two-syllable, three-syllable, and four-syllable states and provinces. In set 14b, there are six each of three-syllable, four-syllable, and five-syllable names.

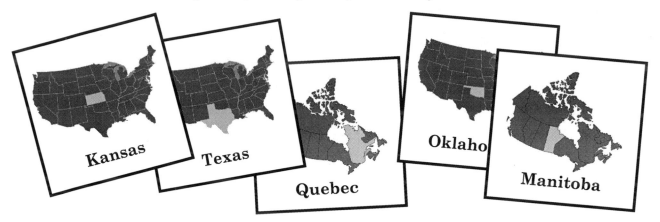

Play: A well-shuffled set of 18 different cards is placed face down in front of each group. At the sound of "Go" one player in each group picks up the top card, pronounces it, and places it face up on the table. From this point on, each player picks up a card, says it, and the group decides which stack it belongs in. according to the number of syllables in the name. When the group has sorted all 18 cards into three stacks, they signal the teacher that they're finished.

Win: In the competitive version, the first group to finish calls out "Finished!" The teacher checks the finishers' solution, and if they're correct the group is declared the winner.

In the non-competitive version, each group completes its stacking and then reads/says the words in their stacks. The other groups listen, and challenge if they want to.

Stress Sort 'n' Stack

The instructions for this game are virtually the same as the instructions above. The difference is that the players sort the cards into three stacks according to which syllable – first, second, third, or fourth receives the heaviest (primary) stress.

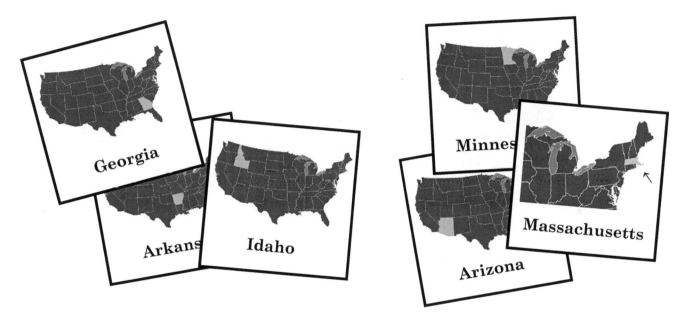

Note: Syllable Sort 'n' Stack is easier than Stress Sort 'n' Stack, and it would be advisable to play the two games in that order. Additional games may be made using Appendixes D and E.

Stress-Match

SPECIAL NOTE: Consult Appendix A for a brief summary of stress in English. The stress-marking system used in this book is:

- – slack - i.e., very little stress
- \\ secondary stress - i.e., medium level
- / primary stress - strongest syllable in a word
- ▮ major stress - strongest syllable in a phrase or sentence
  (With names, the surname gets major stress, and the first name gets primary stress.)

Players: 3-4 in each group.

Level: High Intermediate - Advanced.

Sets: Set 15 only (Presidents).

Cards: There are two kinds of cards in a set: 8 with a president's picture and name, and 8 stress patterns to match the president cards. There are two sets of 8 presidents in the book to allow for two games (or the two sets can be mixed up, to provide greater variety), and in Appendixes F and G there are additional names and patterns which can be used for making more games.

PRESIDENT CARD

MATCHING STRESS PATTERN CARD

1 GEORGE WASHINGTON

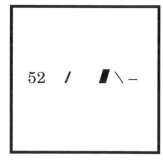

52   /   ▮ \ –

Objective: To sharpen the hearing and production of secondary and primary stress in English. The object of the game is to match the presidents' names with the proper stress pattern. One pattern (/ – ▮ – = Jimmy Carter, Ronald Reagan) is sometimes repeated in a set because it's a common pattern.

Play: Before the game begins, it's necessary to show the president cards and go over the names of the eight presidents in the set so that the students will be somewhat familiar with the stress pattern in the president's name. It may also be necessary to teach how the basic stress levels are marked. One effective way to teach the stress system is to make a set of cards with the names and their stress patterns of well-known people, such as Mick Jagger, Elvis Presley, Marilyn Monroe. This can then be followed up with the less familiar names of the presidents. Each group receives one full set of 16 cards, divided into two stacks, face down: one stack of presidents and one stack of stress patterns. The number of sets needed will depend on the number of groups playing the game.

The students turn over the president cards one at a time and practice saying each president's name. Then they turn over each stress pattern card one at a time and attempt to match it with the appropriate president card. When the group has matched all eight presidents and stress patterns, they call out "Finished!"

Win: In the competitive version, the first group to finish calls out "Finished!" and all play stops. The students call out the numbers on the cards they have matched, and the teacher checks the finishers' solutions. If they're correct the group is declared the winner.

In the non-competitive version, each group completes its matching and then reads/says the numbers in the lower left corner of the two matched cards. The other groups listen, and challenge if they don't agree.

The number matches can be found on the original card pages. They're also listed on the next page.

President and stress card matches

SET 15a	SET 15b
1-52	2-65
3-55	38-64
35-56	33-66
16-50	32-60
39-54	34-68
40-58	28-62
41-53	26-63
36-51	37-61
42-57	5-67

The first number represents the historical sequence of the presidents, for example, Washington was the first president, Kennedy was the 35th. The second number of each match is purely arbitrary.

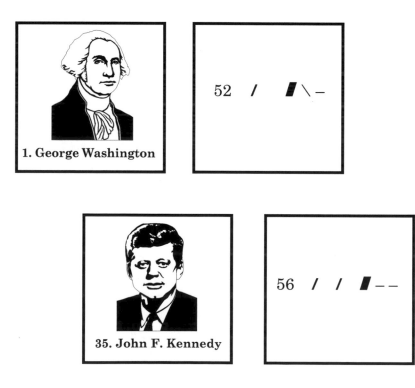

Say It Again

Players: 3-5 in each group.

Level: High Intermediate-Advanced

Sets: Set 16 . One deck of 64 cards for each group. Note that to make one deck you will need four copies of the two pages in set 16. Obviously, if there are several groups, this game requires a lot of cards. Because of that, it is helpful to put each set on different-colored card stock. **Note:** "Liar" is a good preparation for this game.

Cards: A full deck will have 16 subject cards, 16 action cards, 16 place cards, and 16 time cards. Among the four types of cards, each type will have four each of four different cards, for example, four "Oliver Onions," four "Aunt Abigails," etc. The four types correspond to four major syntactic phrases in an English sentence, as indicated below:

Subject Noun Phrase:

Oliver Onion
Aunt Abigail
Polly Pigtails
the Bruise Brothers

Verb Phrase and
Object Noun Phrases:

drive a car
ride a bicycle
walk
take a train

Adverbials of
Direction/Place:

to the office
to/at/on the beach
to/in/from ... to ...
home

Adverbials of Time:

today/yesterday/tomorrow
in the morning/afternoon/evening,
    at night
all week, this week(end), every day
at x o'clock

Objectives: The objective of the game is to play the most cards. The linguistic objective is to practice the placement of major sentence stress (∎) in a normal statement (the last primary-stress syllable in the sentence), and to move major sentence stress to show emphasis (emphatic stress). See Appendix A for additional explanation of word and sentence stress in English. For example, the player first uses the cards in their hand to frame a statement that. uses all four syntactic phrases. This will normally produce sentences with falling intonation and major sentence-level stress on the last primary-stress syllable in each sentence. For example:

/   /–\   /   /   – \ – ∎

Aunt Abigail drove home at two o'**clock**.

SNP   VP ADVL   ADVL

The second objective is for each of the players to make a response that focuses on one of the syntactic phrases and requires the sentence originator to respond by shifting the sentence stress to the phrase that is focused on.

/   / – \ /   /   – \ – ∎

S1: Aunt Abigail drove home at two o' **clock**.

/ – \   ∎   /

S2: Didn't she **walk** home?

/ \   ∎   \

S1: No, she **drove** home.

OR

/   / – \ /   /   – \ – ∎

S1: Aunt Abigail drove home at two o' **clock**.

/ \   / – –   ∎ –   \   \

S3: I thought Oliver **On**ion did that.

∎ / \   /   ∎ – \   \   \

S1: No, I said Aunt **Ab**igail drove home.

Deal: Eight cards to each player. The remainder are placed face down in a pile in the center as the discard/pick-up deck.

Pre-play: Because the instructions are somewhat complicated, it's a good idea to select a group of four and walk them through one round of play as the others watch and ask questions.

Play: The player to the left of the dealer starts the game.

1. The player frames a sentence using all four phrases. For example:

Oliver Onion / took the train / to Kalamazoo / yesterday.

The player pronounces the sentence and lays it out in front for the others to see. The player then picks up four cards from the discard/pick-up pile to replace those they played. If the player can't frame a sentence because they are lacking a card from one of the phrases, they call out "Pass" and return up to four cards to the bottom of the discard/pick-up deck and pick up the same number of cards from the top of the deck.

2. After the first player has put down the sentence, each other player in turn responds to one part of the phrase and simultaneously plays the appropriate phrase cards from their own hand and picks up one card from the discard/pick-up pile. The typical response will be a negative question.

      S1: Oliver Onion took the train to Kalamazoo yesterday.
      S2: (playing an appropriate phrase card — the automobile)
          Didn't he **drive** to Kalamazoo?
      S1: No, he **took the train** (to Kalamazoo).

Players are not required to respond, and as the game comes down to the last few hands, this could be a good tactic because the player is holding one card of each type and can lay them all down in the next turn.

3. The first player then counter-responds, as in the example above, with the stress on the phrase that is focused on.

4. The play then moves to the player to the left of the first player, and so on.

5. The game ends when one player uses all their cards or no player can construct a sentence or pass because the discard/pick-up pile is empty.

Win: The player with the largest number of played cards is the winner.

Word and Sentence Stress

As we speak English, some of the syllables in a word, or some of the words in a phrase or sentence, will be spoken with more force than others:

FOUR of the **SYL**lables in this **SENT**ence are **LOUD**.

We automatically turn up the volume as we utter stressed (loud) syllables. At the same time, as the syllable becomes louder, it also tends to become longer in duration and higher in pitch.

SIX   **SYL**   **SENT**   **LOUD, LONG,**   **HIGH.**
   of the   lables in this   ence are   and

In English, stressed syllables tend to crowd out the other syllables, which are consequently spoken more quietly and quickly. In the word "syllable," (**syl**-la-ble), the first syllable is stressed, and the other two syllables are not stressed. As this happens, there is a strong tendency for the unstressed vowels to change into an "uh" sound, a vowel sound called "schwa." This process is called **reduction**, and it occurs in most multi-syllable words and in most long phrases and sentences.

Now compare and say:

/
noun

/ \
pronoun

– /
pronounce

– \ \ / –
pronunciation

The first word, "noun," is a single-syllable word. It has **primary stress** (/) because every word spoken in isolation (not as part of a longer phrase or sentence) must have a strong, or primary stress on one syllable. The next word, "pronoun," is stressed heavily on the first syllable, but the second syllable is not completely reduced. It still has some stress, and the vowel is not reduced to "ə" This is called **secondary stress.**

In the verb, "pronounce," the vowel in the first syllable is reduced to the point of becoming "uh." This example shows that when stress is weak, the vowel tends to lose its identity to become the short, weak, unstressed schwa.

Now look at the word "pronunciation." The syllable "a" receives the primary stress, but "nun" also receives some stress — secondary stress. "Pro" and "tion" are spoken quickly and quietly with only weak stress, and the vowels are reduced to "uh."

In summary, words can have three levels of stress: primary (/), secondary (\) and weak (–).

When several words are strung together as a phrase or sentence, this group of words acts somewhat like a single word. One syllable in the group will receive heavier stress than the other syllables in the group. In a normal statement sentence, the final stressed syllable in the sentence will receive the heaviest stress. This is **major phrase / sentence stress**, marked with a heavy slash (❙).

However, major sentence stress doesn't always occur on the final stressed syllable in a sentence. This happens when the speaker wants to focus attention on some other word in the sentence for emphasis or contrast. In the games "Dominoes," "Liar," and "Say it Again," **emphatic stress** is used to contrast something in one sentence with something in another, usually previous, sentence:

                                ❙
        " I have a big heart in a circle."
                            ❙
        "And I have a **SMALL** heart in a circle."

In the "Stress-Match" game, names are spoken as a phrase that acts like a sentence, so that the strongest syllable in the surname (last name) receives primary sentence stress:

            /   ❙ \   –
        George Washington.

But if the first president's name were placed in a sentence, it would lose its ❙:

        /   /   \   –   –   –   \   /   – –   – –   \ /–   ❙
        George Washington was the first president of the United States.

Sound and Spelling Chart

The sounds in dark (bold) type are practiced in this book. When the sound is in the book, the sample words are pictured on cards. The spelling of the sound is underlined.

Vowels

Sound	Spellings	Sound	Spellings
iy	sheep, meat	i	ship
ey	paper, pain	e	pen, head
æ	pan, axe	ə	cup
a	pot	au	caught, fall
u	put, book	uw	tool, rule
ow	go, slow	oy	boy, avoid
ay	bite, try	aw	loud, clown
er	her, word, bird	yuw	few, music

Consonants

Sound	Spellings	Sound	Spellings
p	pan	**b**	ban
t	tent	**d**	duck
k	coat, tack	**g**	goat, tag
f	fan	v	van
th	thumb, mouth	*th*	leather
s	sink, peace	z	zinc, peas
sh	shop, dish	zh	pleasure
ch	chop, ditch	j	jam
m	sum, mouse	n	sun, gnat
h	how	ng	sing, thank
l	lice, heel	r	rice
w	will	y	you

Problem Areas for Specific Languages

The sets listed below are recommended for students from the following language backgrounds:

Arabic: Sets 2, 3, 7, 8, 12, 14

Chinese: Sets 1, 2, 3, 4, 5, 6, 7, 8, 11, 12, 13, 14, 15, 16

Czech: Sets 2, 4, 5, 8, 10, 12, 15, 16

Farsi: Sets 1, 2, 5, 8, 13, 14, 15, 16

French: Sets 1, 3, 4, 5, 8, 9, 10, 12, 13, 14, 15, 16

German: Sets 2, 3, 8, 10, 12

Greek: Sets 1, 2, 5, 9, 10, 15, 16

Haitian: Sets 1, 3, 4, 5, 8, 9, 10, 12, 13, 14, 15, 16

Hungarian: Sets 1, 2, 5, 8, 12, 15

Italian: Sets 1, 2, 4, 8, 11, 12, 16

Japanese: Sets 1, 4, 6, 7, 8, 13, 16

Korean: Sets 1, 3, 6, 7, 8, 12, 13, 16

Polish: Sets 2, 3, 5, 7, 8, 12, 14, 15, 16

Portuguese: Sets 1, 2, 4, 8, 9, 12, 14, 15, 16

Russian: Sets 1, 2, 7, 8, 12, 15, 16

Serbo-Croatian: Sets 1, 2, 4, 5, 8, 12, 15, 16

Spanish: Sets 1, 3, 4, 7, 8, 9, 10, 11, 12, 13, 14, 15, 16

Thai: Sets 6, 7, 8, 9, 11, 12, 13, 14, 15, 16

Turkish: Sets 1, 2, 8, 12, 13, 15, 16

Vietnamese: Sets 7, 8, 13, 14, 15, 16

Additional States, Provinces, and Other Places

This list of additions to Set 14 is included for anyone wishing to construct more games. There are 44 place names on this list. The number in parentheses indicates which syllable gets the heaviest stress.

1 Syllable
Guam (1)
Maine (1)

2 Syllables
Yukon (1)
Cape Cod (2)
New York (2)
Great Plains (2)

3 Syllables
Washington (1)
Iowa (1)
Labrador (1)
Michigan (1)
Florida (1)
Newfoundland (1) or (2)
Alaska (2)
Nevada (2)
Montana (2)
Wyoming (2)
Nebraska (2)
New England (2)
Missouri (2)
Rhode Island (2)
New Hampshire (2)
Virginia (2)
Tennessee (3)
Hudson Bay (3)

4 Syllables
the Everglades (2)
California (3)
Puerto Rico (3)
North Dakota (3)
Pennsylvania (3)
South Dakota (3)
Indiana (3)
Alabama (3)
West Virginia (3)

5 Syllables
Gulf of Mexico (3)
Mojave Desert (4)
the Virgin Islands (4)
the Rocky Mountains (4)

6 Syllables
Northwest Territories (3)
the Tennessee Valley (5)
Okefenokee Swamp (6)

7 Syllables
the Bermuda Triangle (5)
American Samoa (6)

8 Syllables
the Oklahoma Panhandle (6)
the District of Columbia (6)

Cities

This list of additons to Set 14 is included for anyone wishing to construct more games. There are 36 place names on this list . The number in parentheses indicates which syllable gets the heaviest stress.

2 Syllables

Houston (1)
Phoenix (1)
Dallas (1)
Saint John (2)
Detroit (2)
Memphis (1)
Boston (1)
Denver (1)
Richmond (1)
Saint Paul (2)
Fort Worth (2)
Quebec (2)

3 Syllables

Montreal (3)
Calgary (1)
Ottawa (1)
Toronto (2)
San Jose (3)
Baltimore (1)
Jacksonville (1)
Miami (2)
Saint Louis (2)
Chicago (2)
El Paso (2)
Tacoma (2)

4 Syllables

San Francisco (3)
Los Angeles (2)
San Diego (3)
Kansas City (3)
Albuquerque (1)
Honolulu (3)
Sacramento (3)
Jersey City (3)
Corpus Christi (3)
Salt Lake City (3)
Winston-Salem (3)
Cincinnati (3)

Additional Presidents

#	Name	Pattern		
4	James Madison	/	▰ – –	
6	John Quincy Adams	/	/ \	▰ –
7	Andrew Jackson	/ \	▰ –	
8	Martin Van Buren	/ –	\	▰ –
9	William Henry Harrison	/ –	/ \	▰ – –
10	John Tyler	/	▰ –	
11	James K. Polk	/	/	▰
12	Zachary Taylor	/ – \	▰ –	
13	Millard Fillmore	/ –	▰ \	
14	Franklin Pierce	/ –	▰	
15	James Buchanan	/	\ ▰ –	
17	Andrew Johnson	/ \	▰ –	
18	Ulysses S. Grant	\ / \	/	▰
19	Rutherford B. Hayes	/ – –	/	▰
20	James Garfield	/	▰ \	
21	Chester A. Arthur	/ –	/	▰ –
22 & 24	Grover Cleveland	/ –	▰ –	
23	Benjamin Harrison	/ – –	▰ – –	
25	William McKinley	/ –	– ▰ \	
27	William Howard Taft	/ –	/ –	▰
29	Warren Harding	/ –	▰ \	
30	Calvin Coolidge	/ –	▰ –	
31	Herbert Hoover	/ –	▰ –	

NOTES:

1. Grover Cleveland, Calvin Coolidge, and Herbert Hoover have the same pattern (/ – ▰ –).

2. Andrew Jackson, Andrew Johnson, Warren Harding, and Millard Fillmore have the same pattern (/ \ ▰ –).

Women Writers

Name	Pattern		
Emily Dickinson	/ – \	▰ – –	
Harriet Beecher Stowe	/ – –	/ –	▰
Amy Tan	/ \	▰	
Eudora Welty	\ / –	▰ \	
Sarah Orne Jewett	/ –	/	▰ –
Alice Walker	/ –	▰ –	
Pearl S. Buck	/	/	▰
Louisa May Alcott	\ /–	/	▰ \
Alice Munro	/ –	\ ▰	
Carson McCullers	/ –	– ▰ –	
Katherine Anne Porter	/ –	/	▰ \
Dorothy Parker	/ – \	▰ –	

MEN WRITERS

Name	Pattern		
Jack London	/	▮ –	
Edgar Allan Poe	/ –	/ –	▮
Robert Frost	/ –	▮	
Ernest Hemingway	/ –	▮ \ /	
Robert Service	/ –	▮ –	
Herman Melville	/ –	▮ \	
Saul Bellow	/	▮ \	
Farley Mowatt	/ \	▮ –	
J. D. Salinger	/	/	▮ – –
Tom Wolfe	/	▮	
E. L. Doctorow	/	/	▮ – \
James A. Michener	/	/	▮ \

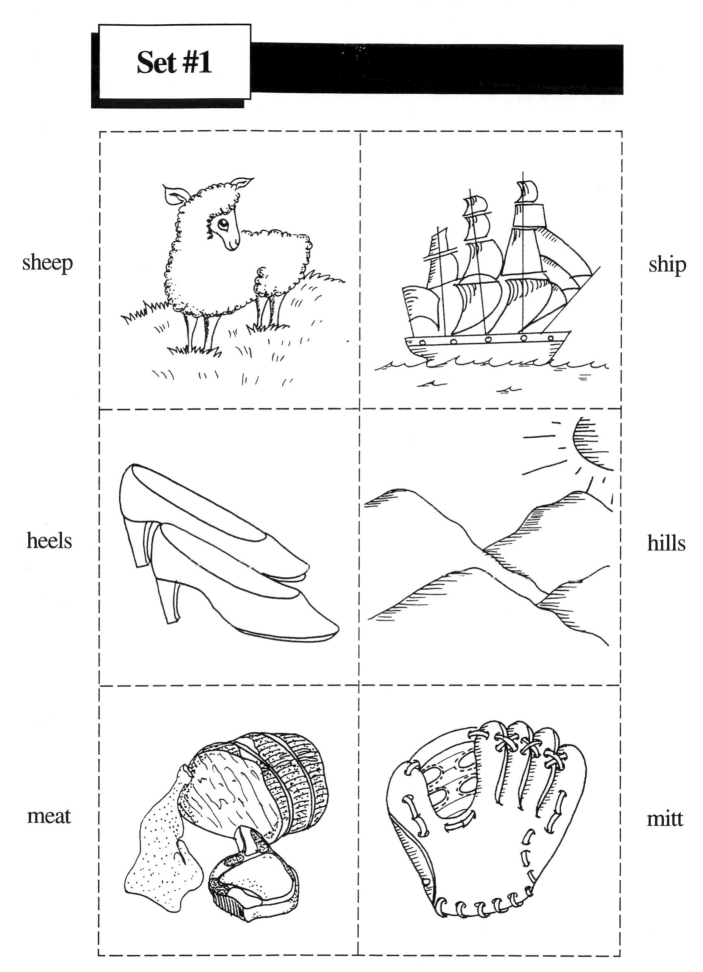

sheep

ship

heels

hills

meat

mitt

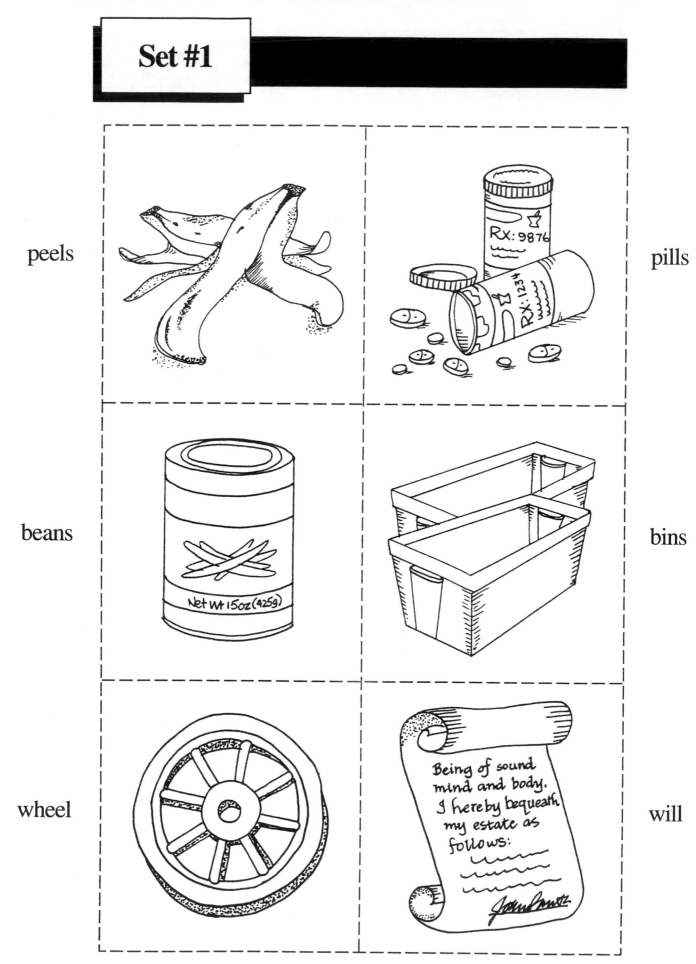

peels

pills

beans

bins

wheel

will

leap

lip

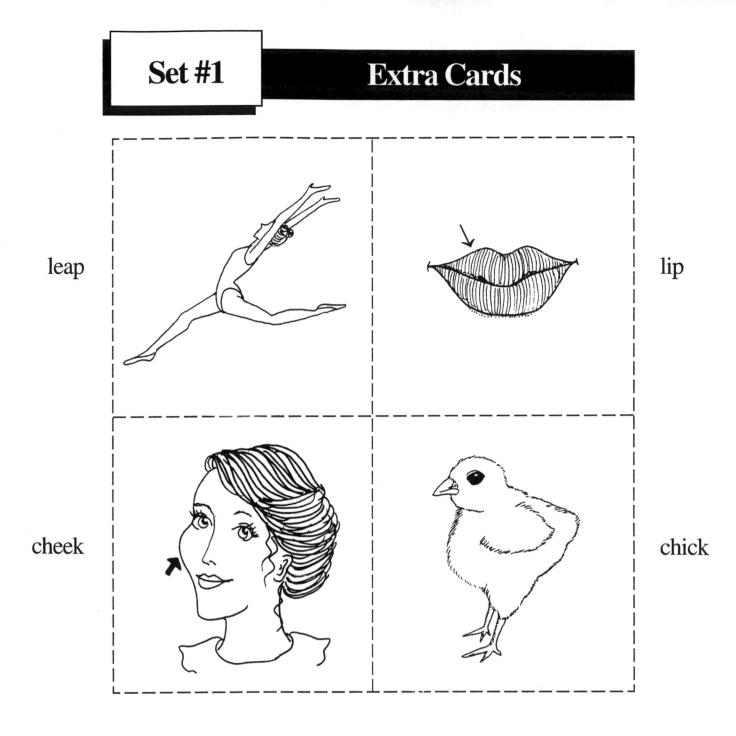

cheek

chick

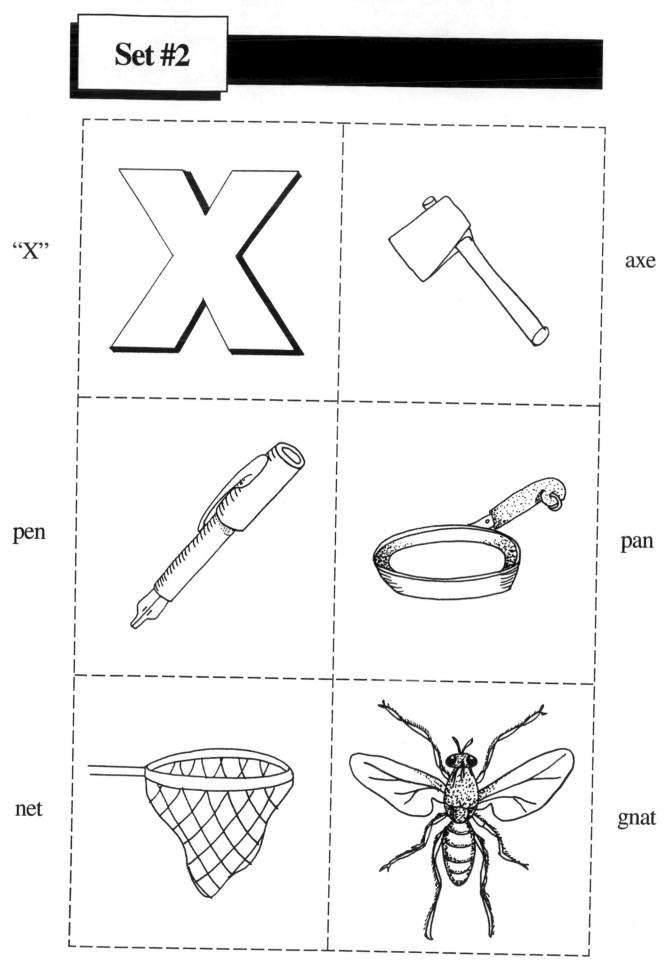

"X"

axe

pen

pan

net

gnat

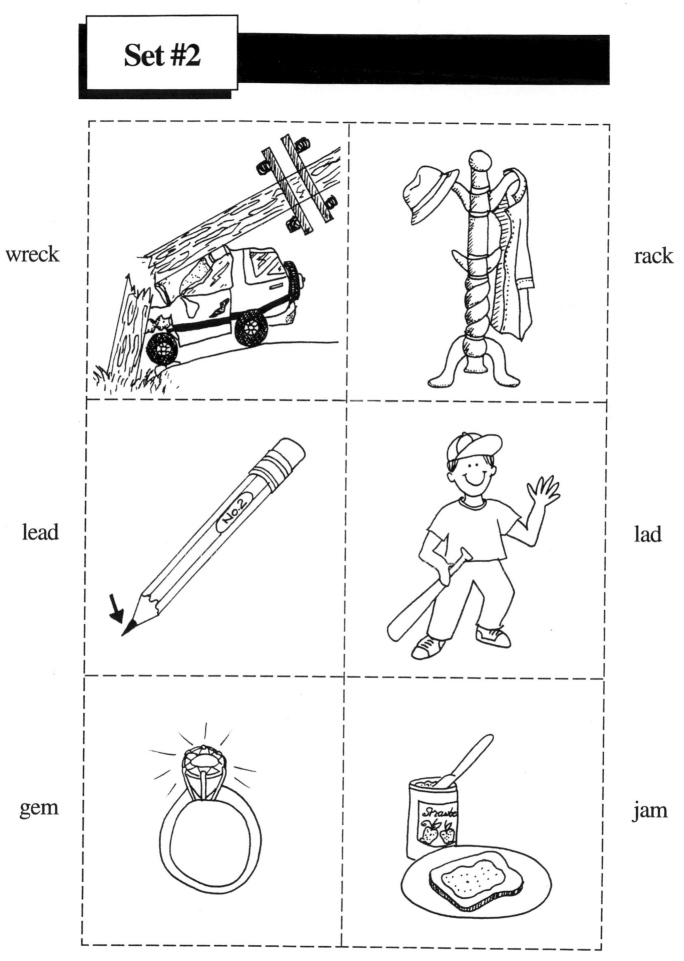

wreck

rack

lead

lad

gem

jam

pedal

paddle

hem

ham

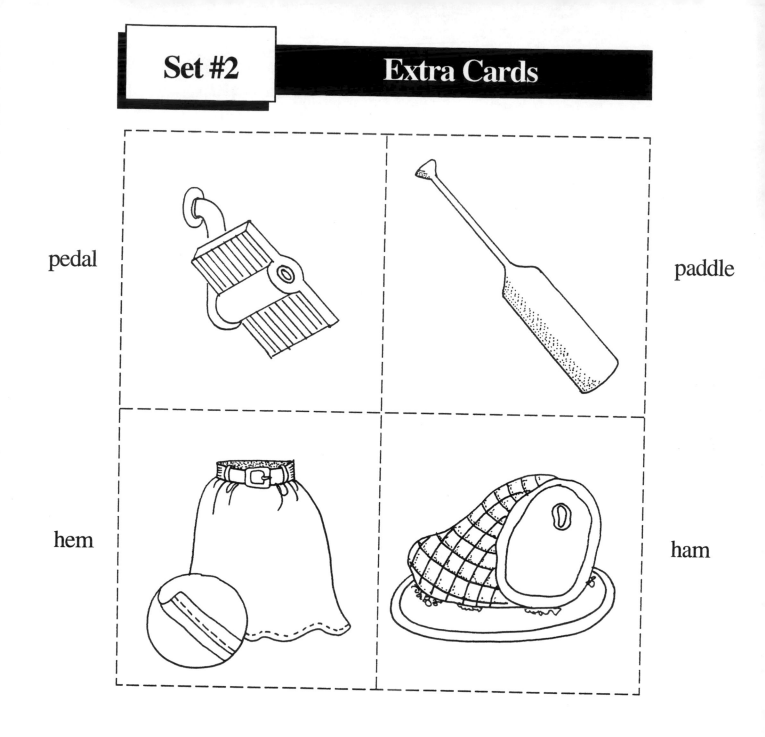

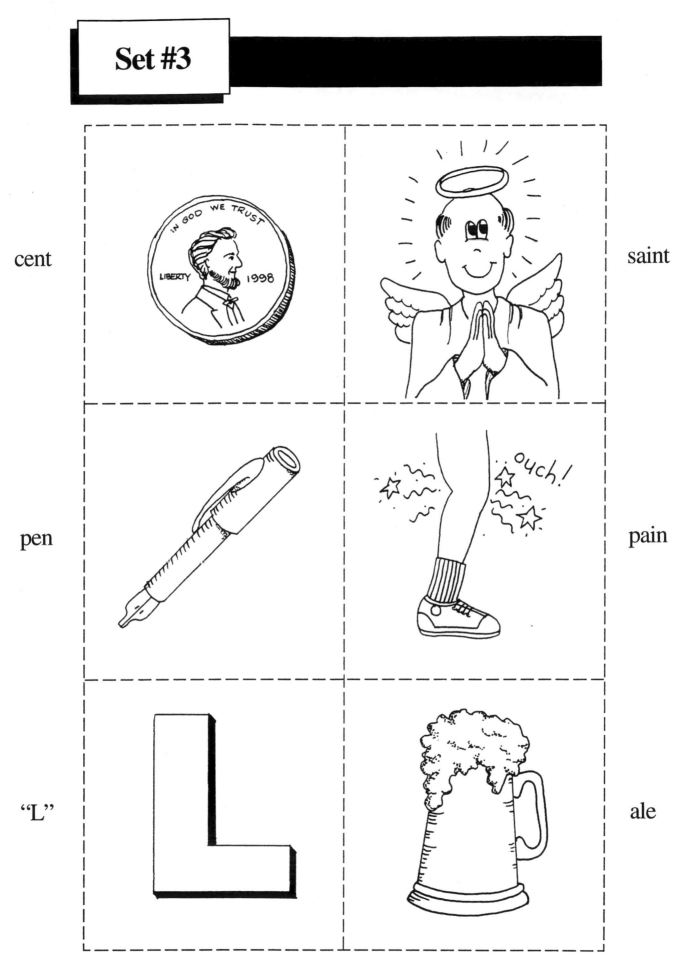

cent

saint

pen

pain

"L"

ale

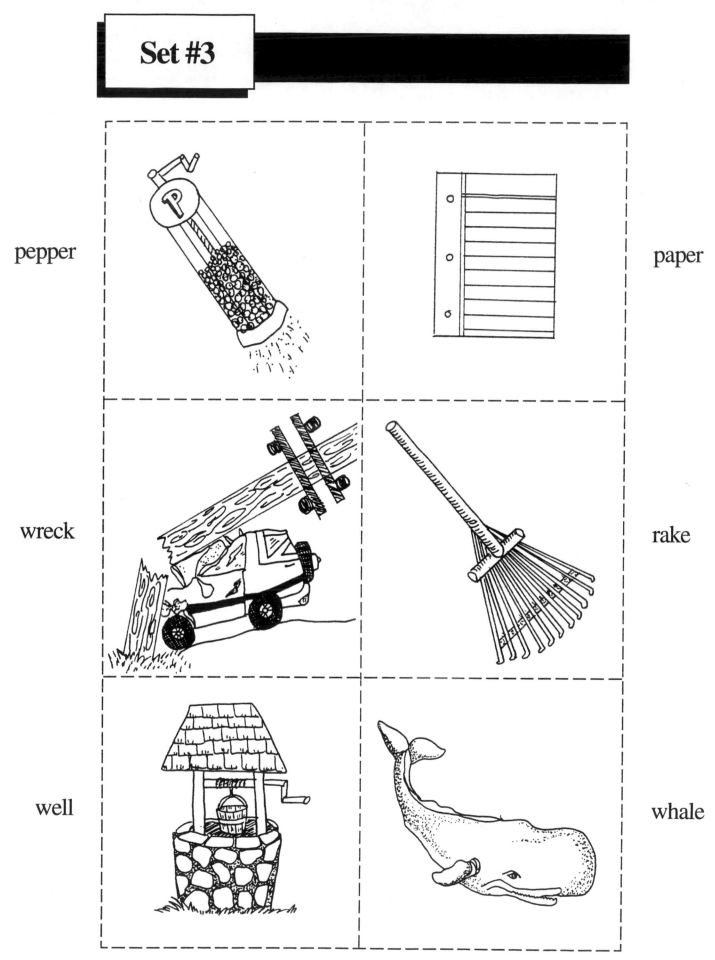

pepper

paper

wreck

rake

well

whale

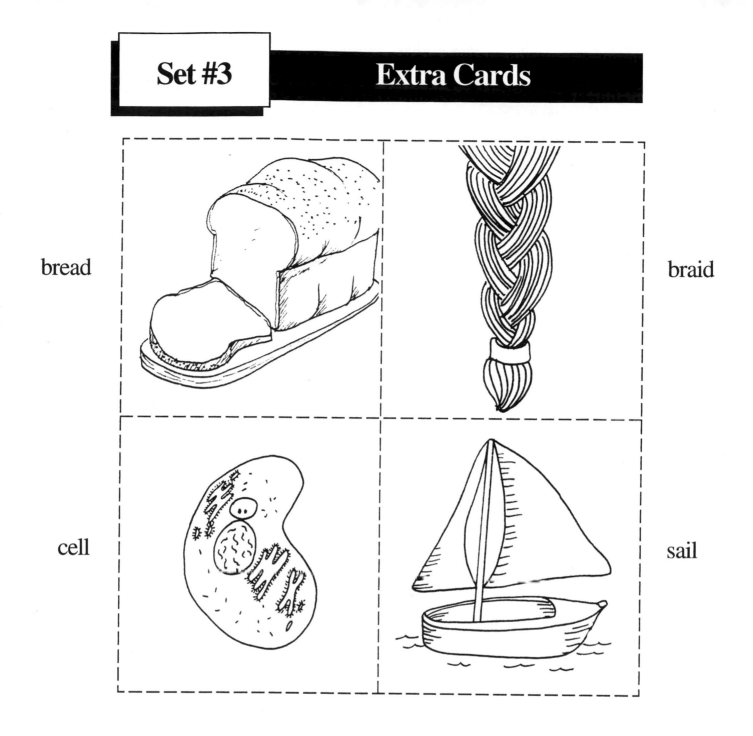

bread

braid

cell

sail

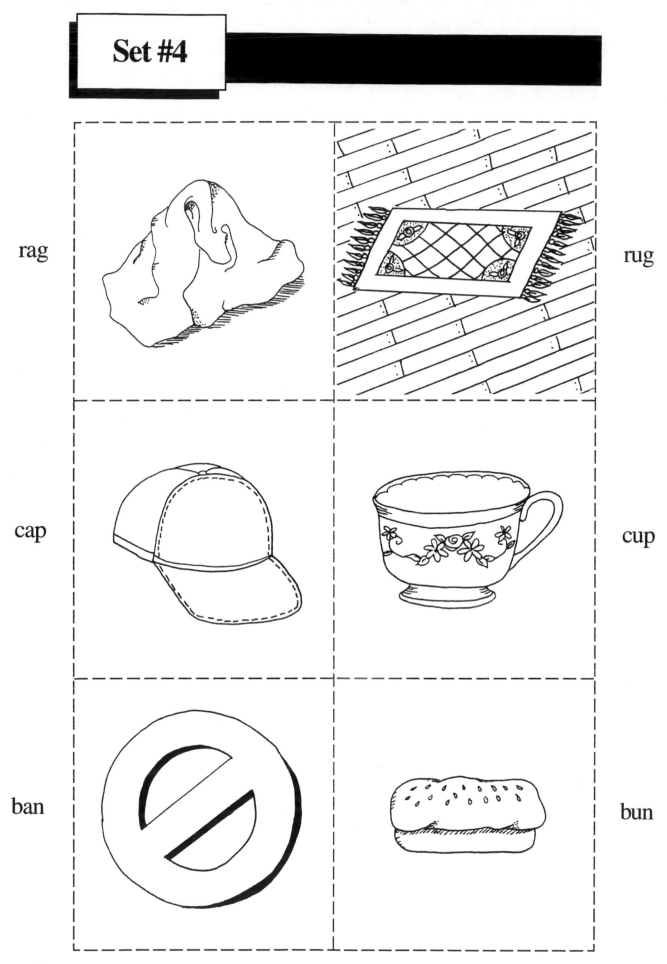

rag

rug

cap

cup

ban

bun

Set #4

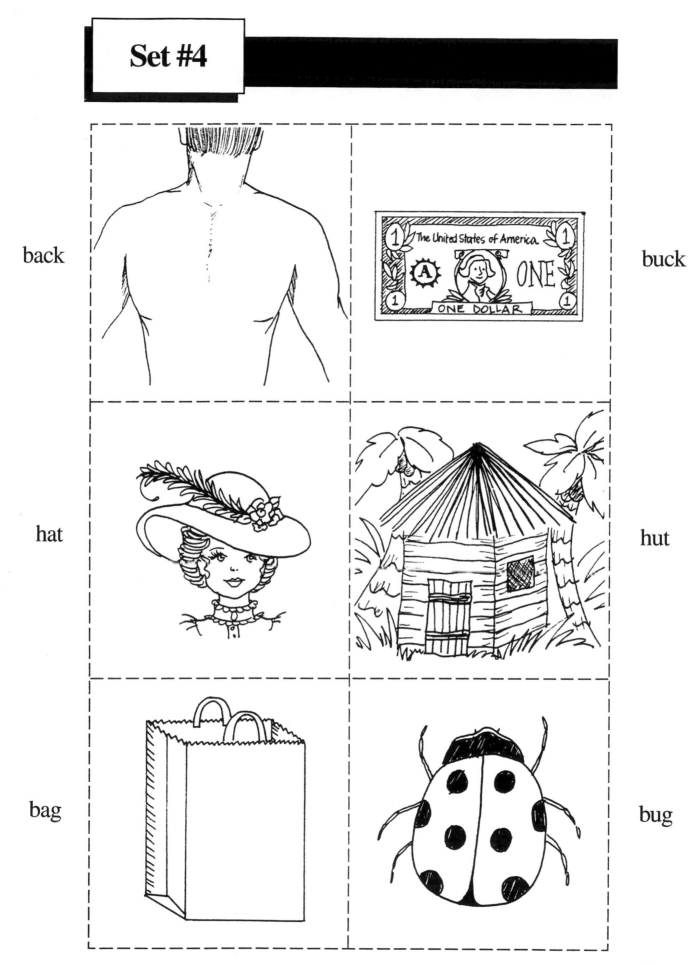

back

buck

hat

hut

bag

bug

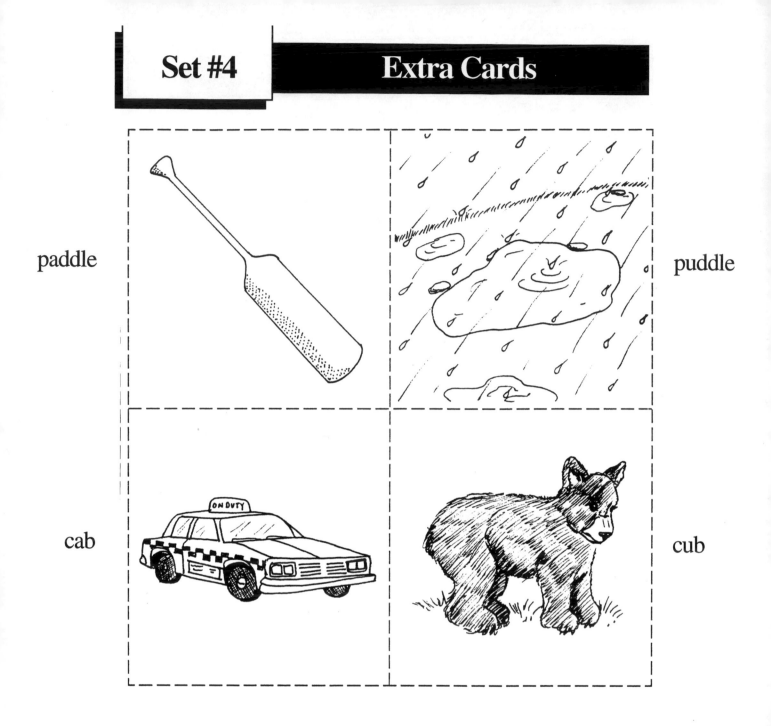

paddle

puddle

cab

cub

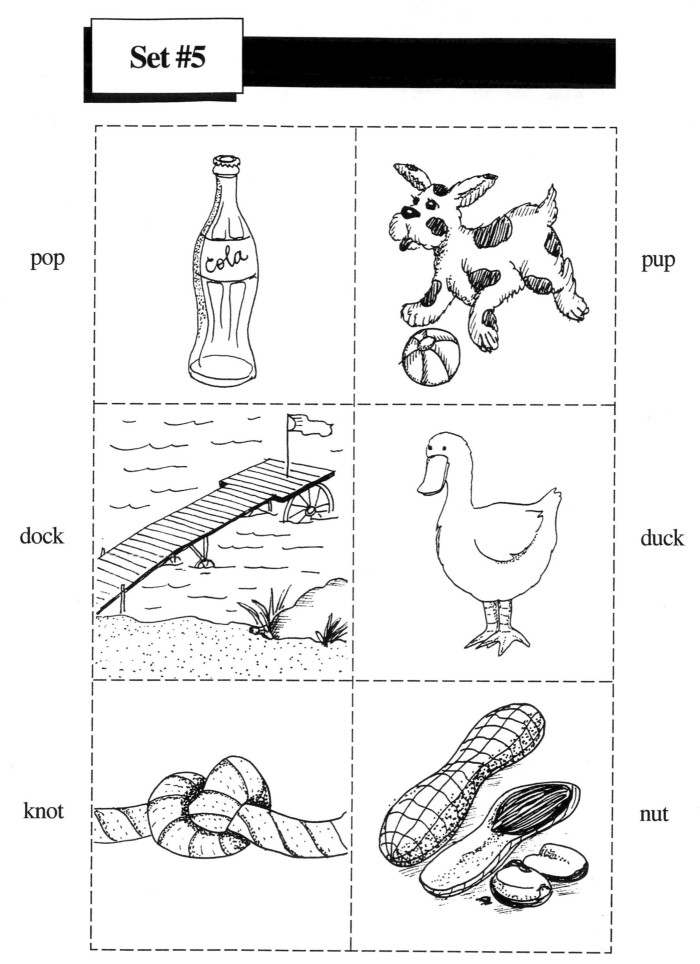

pop

pup

dock

duck

knot

nut

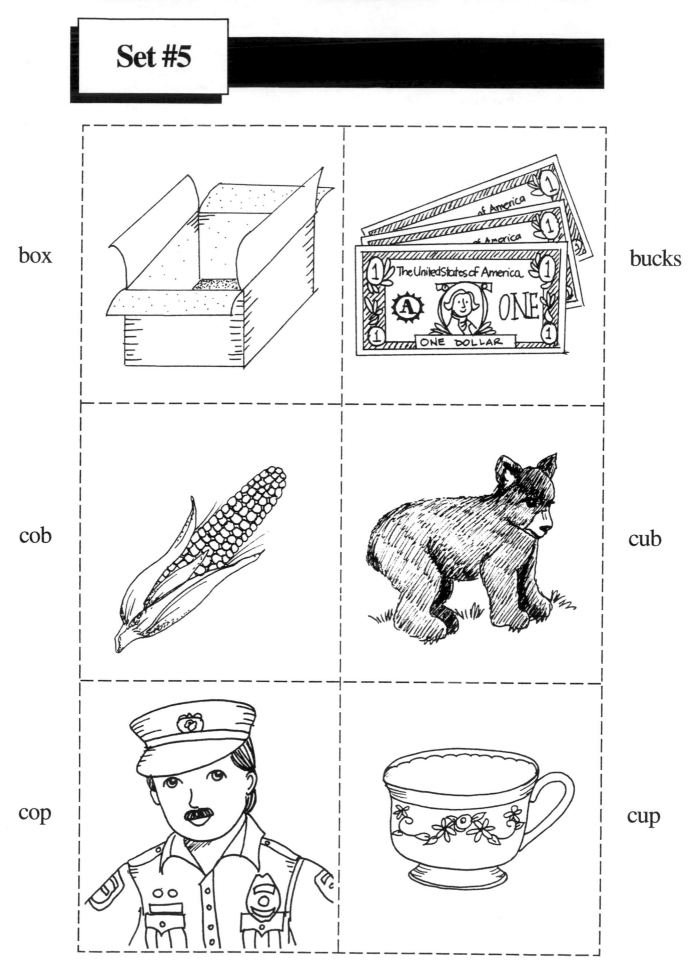

box

bucks

cob

cub

cop

cup

bomb

bum

pot

putt

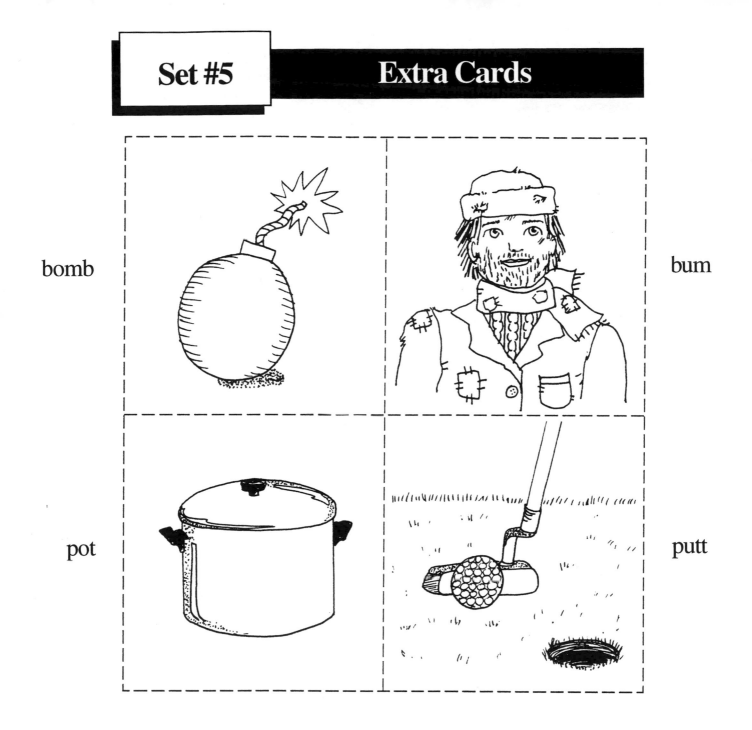

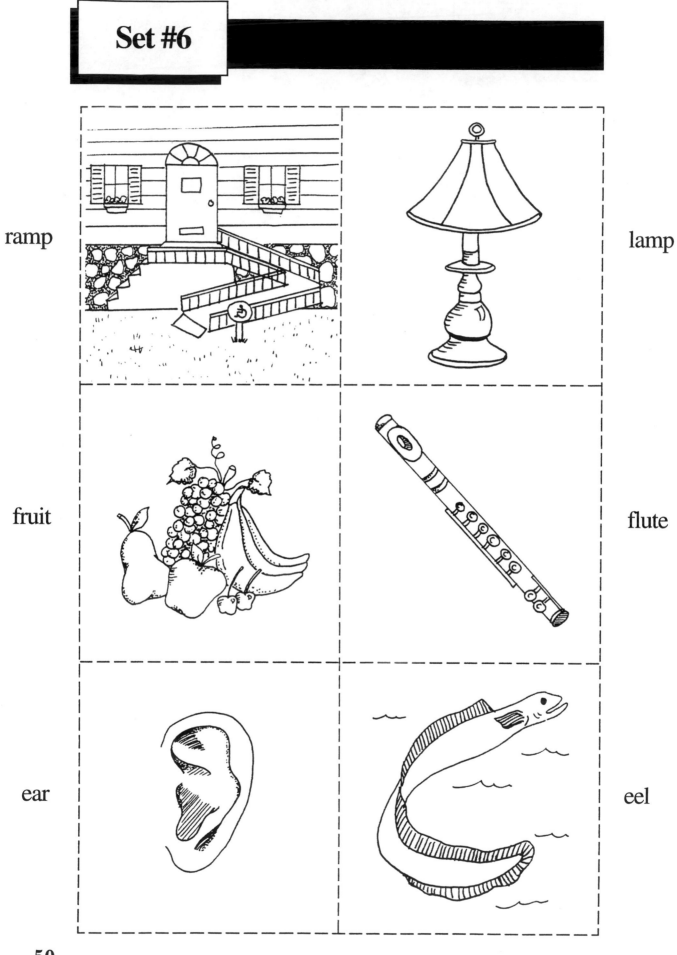

ramp

lamp

fruit

flute

ear

eel

Set #6

grass

glass

fire

file

pear

pail

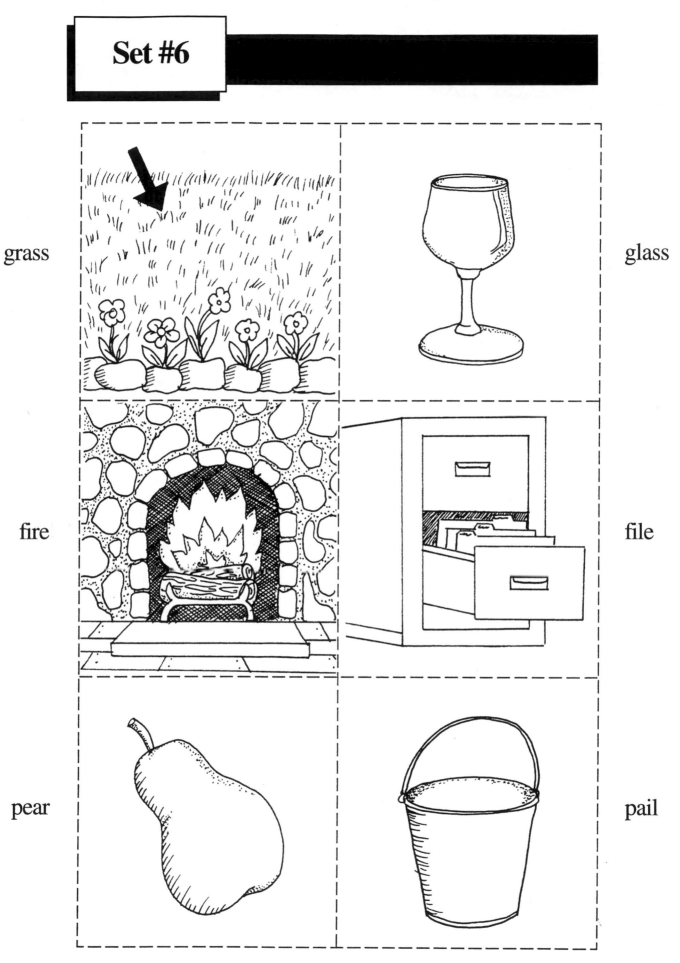

rice

lice

rake

lake

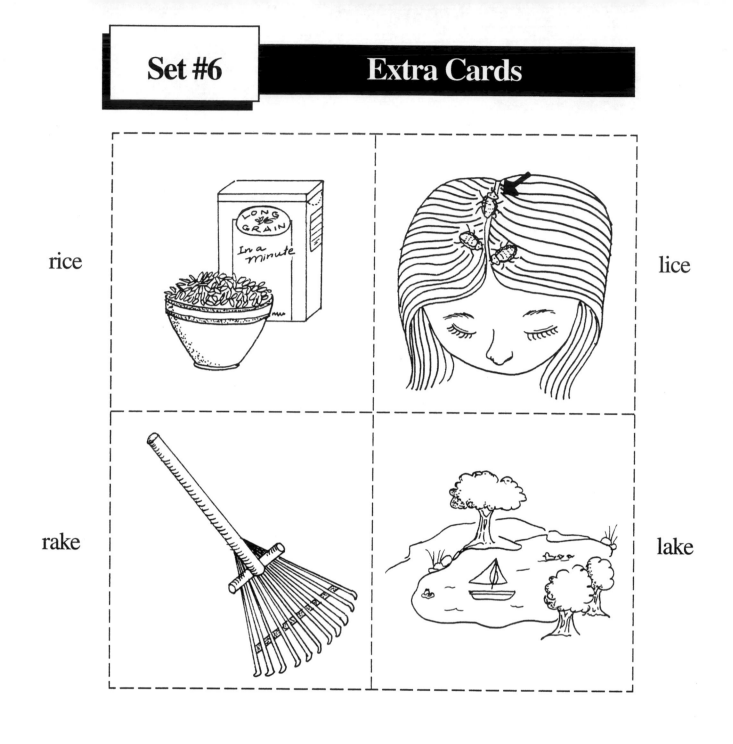

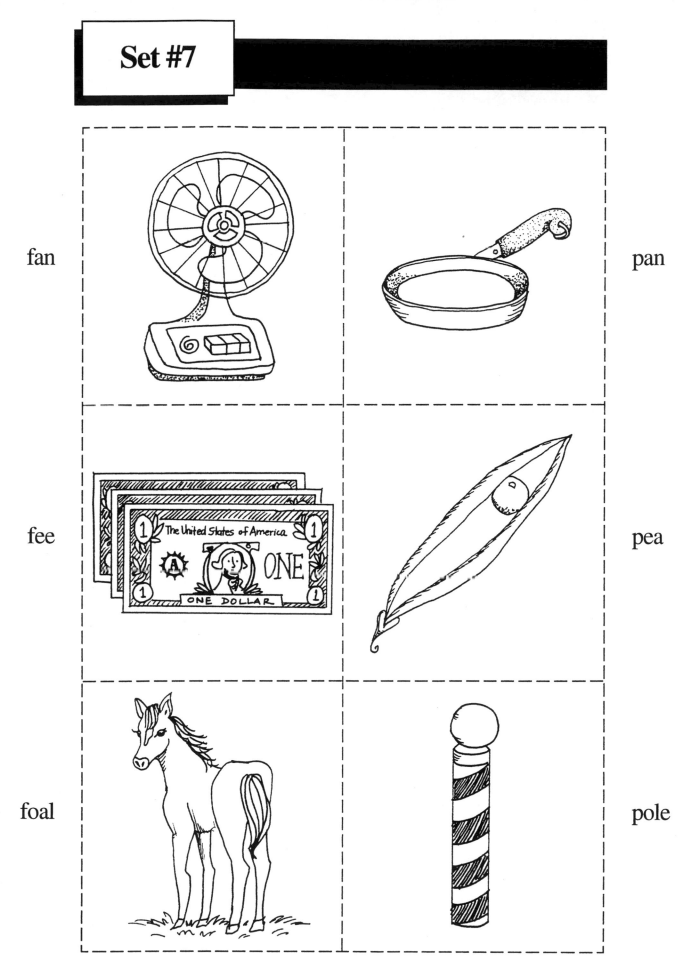

fan

pan

fee

pea

foal

pole

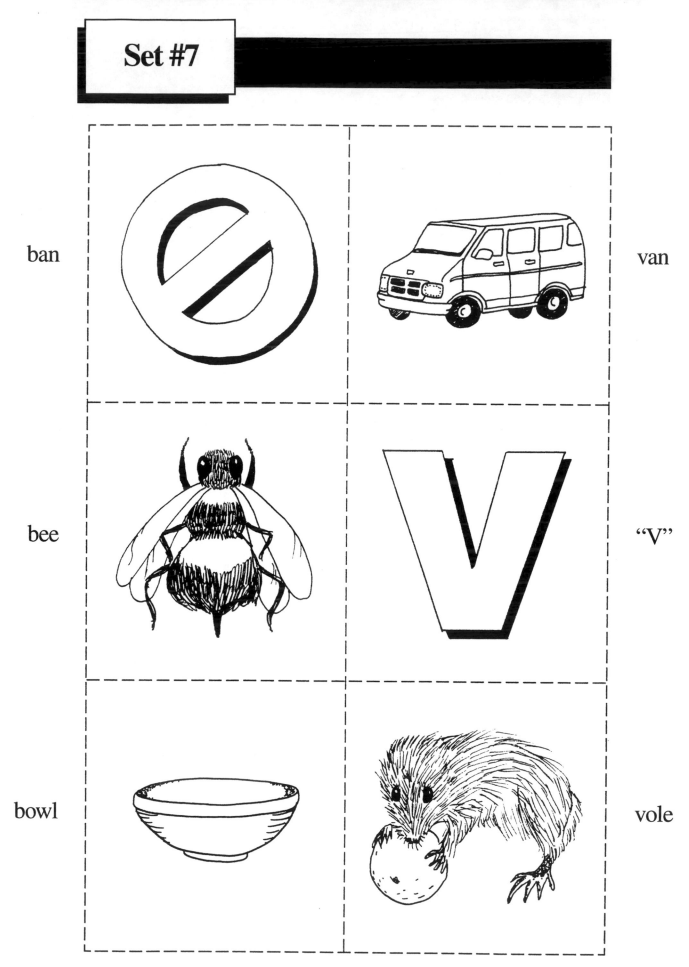

ban

van

bee

"V"

bowl

vole

pace

face

vase

base

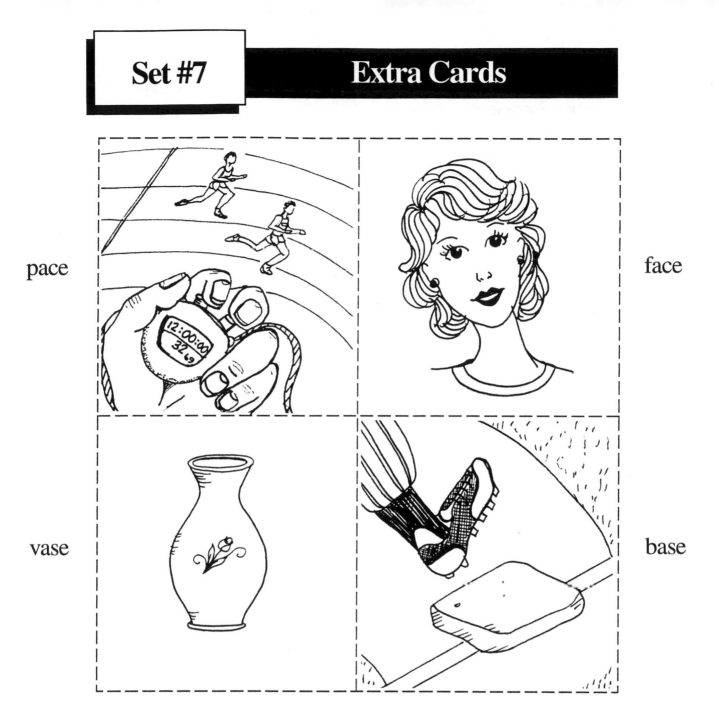

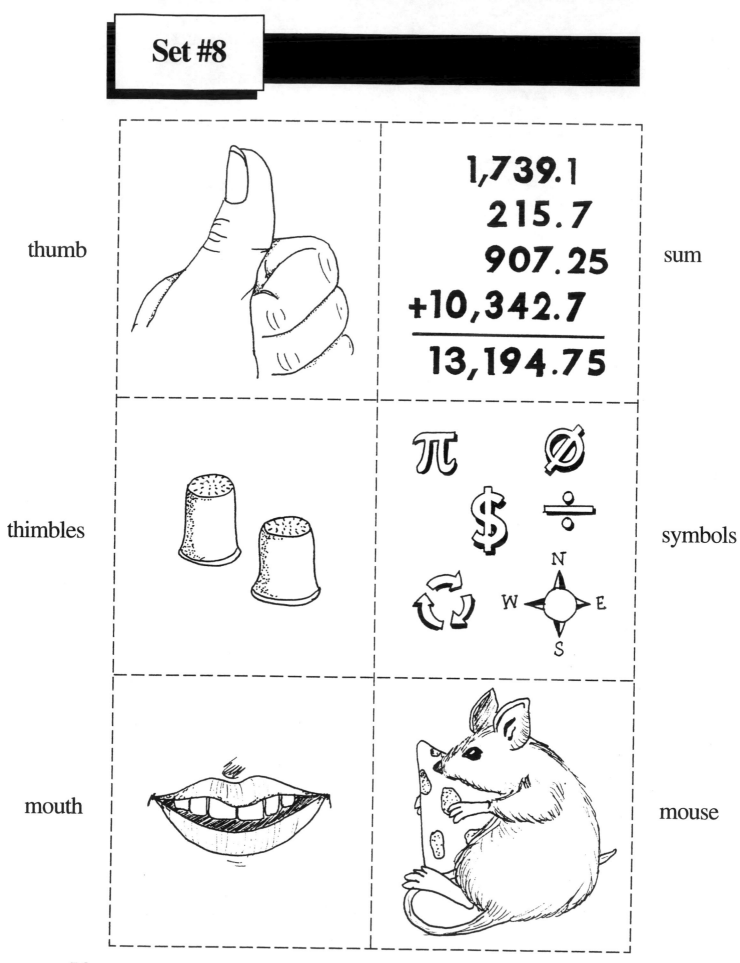

thumb

$$\begin{array}{r} 1{,}739.1 \\ 215.7 \\ 907.25 \\ +10{,}342.7 \\ \hline 13{,}194.75 \end{array}$$

sum

thimbles

symbols

mouth

mouse

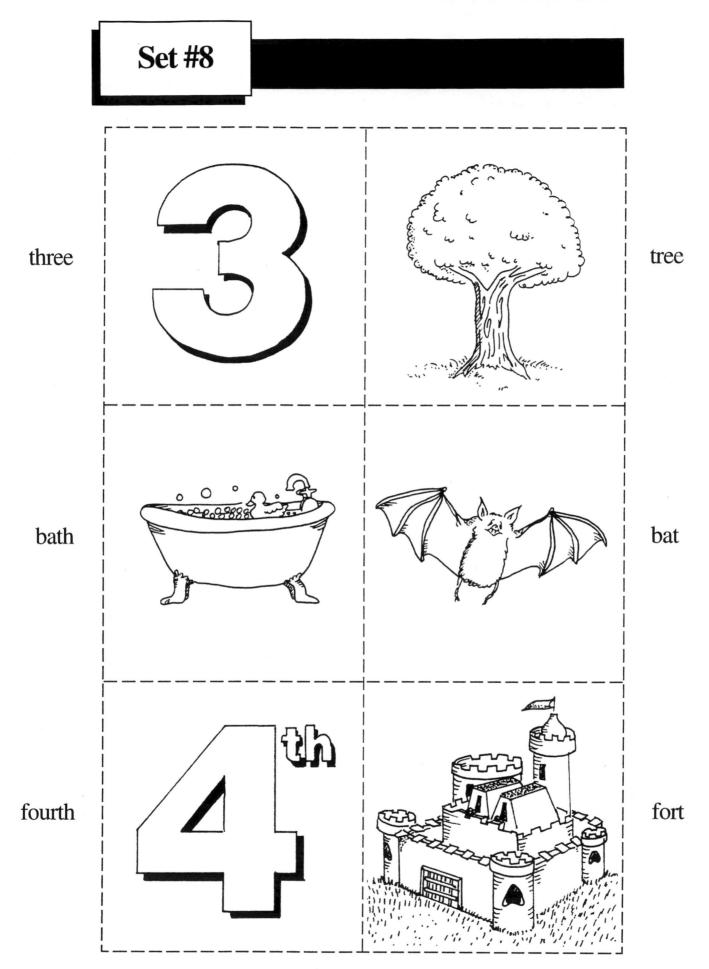

three

tree

bath

bat

fourth

fort

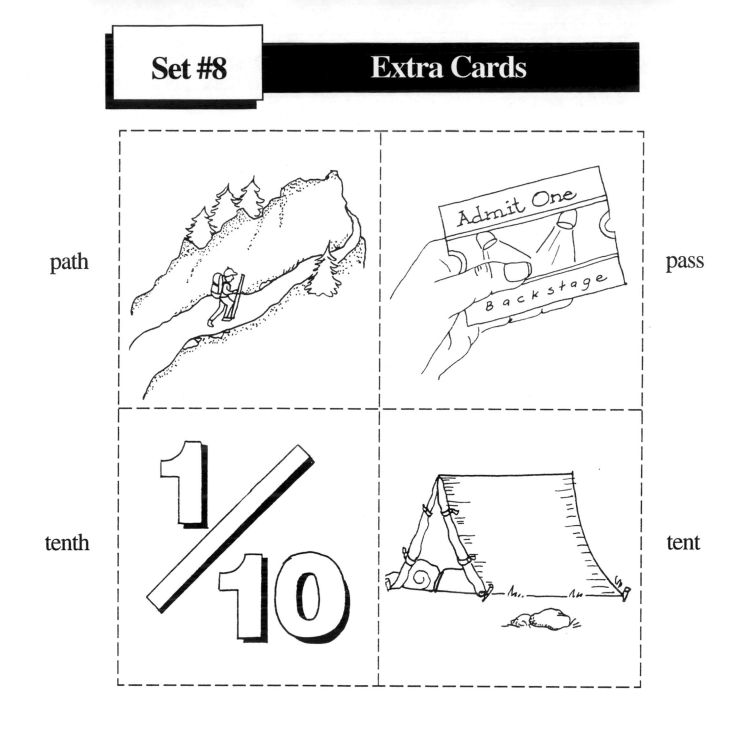

path

pass

tenth

tent

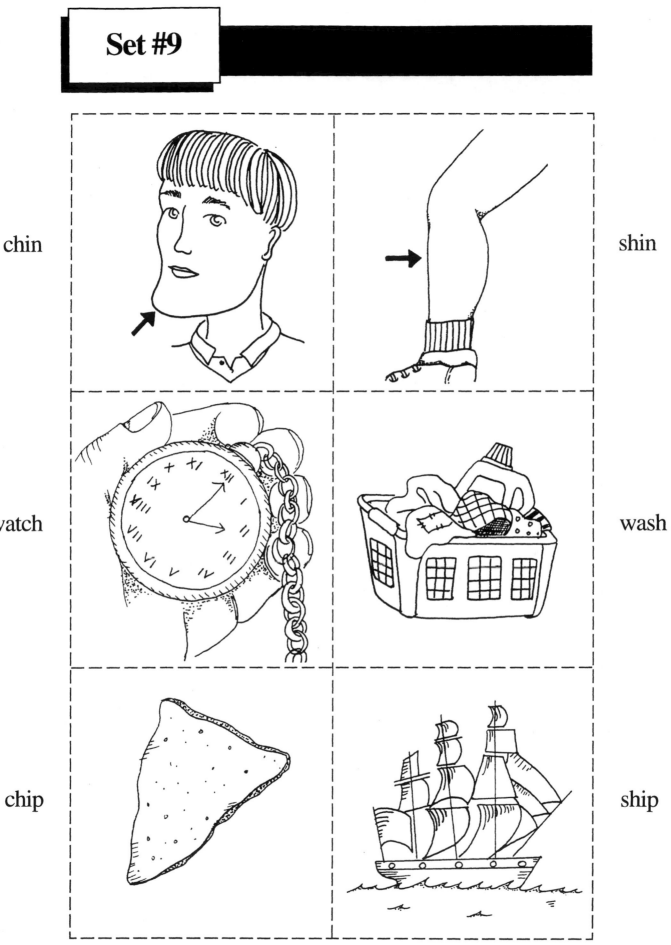

chin

shin

watch

wash

chip

ship

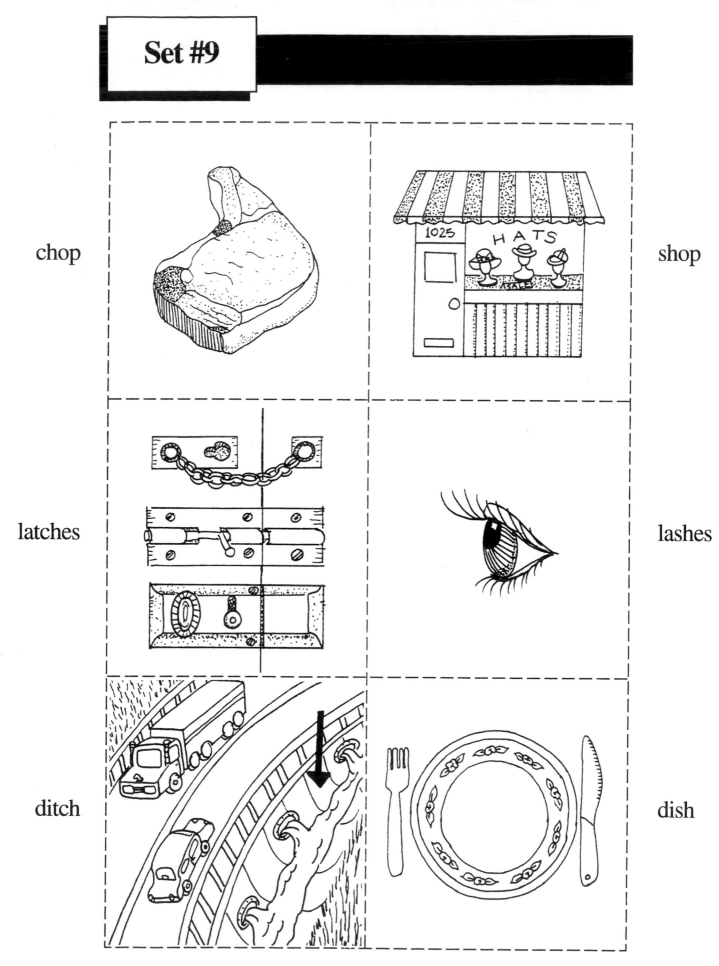

chop

shop

latches

lashes

ditch

dish

witch

wish

cherry

sherry

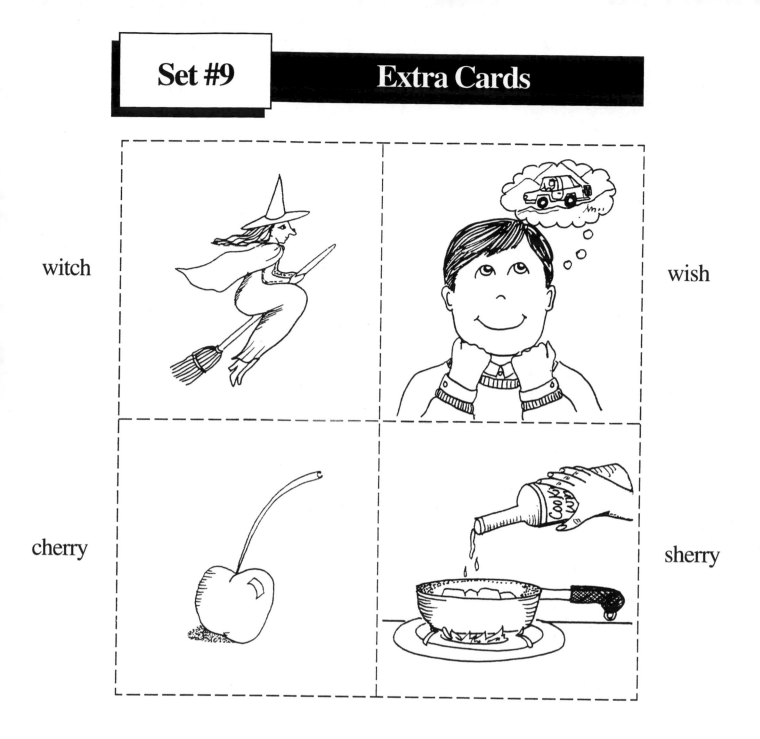

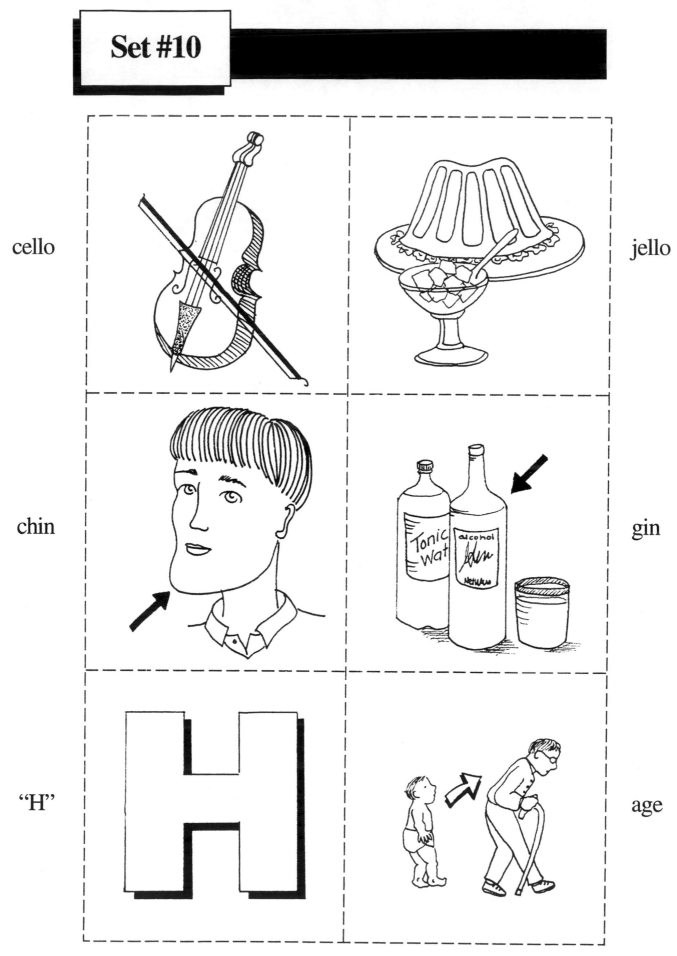

cello

jello

chin

gin

"H"

age

Set #10

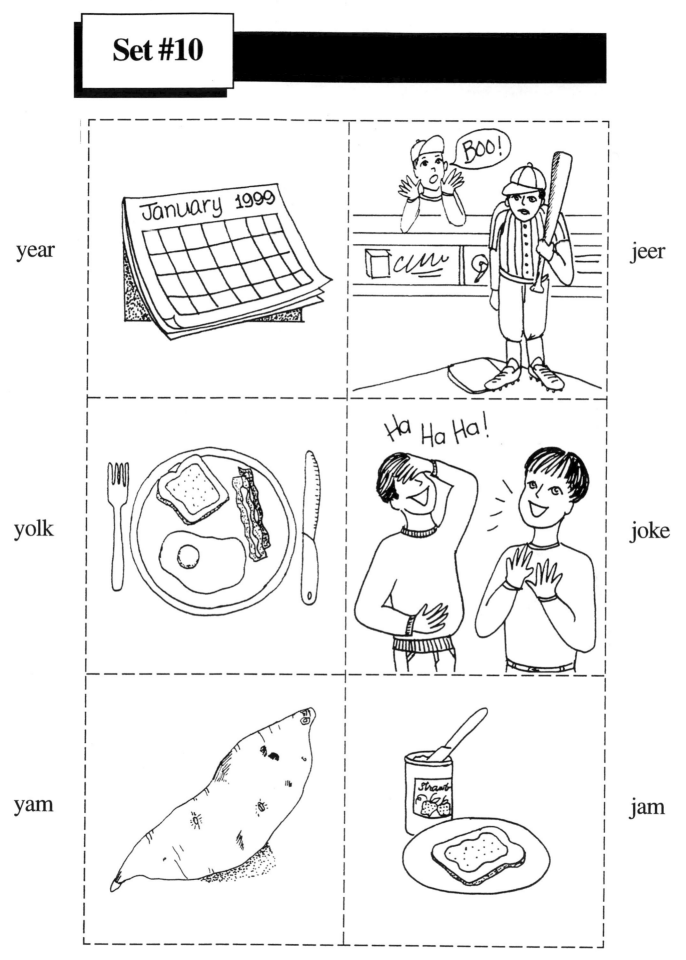

year

jeer

yolk

joke

yam

jam

Yale

jail

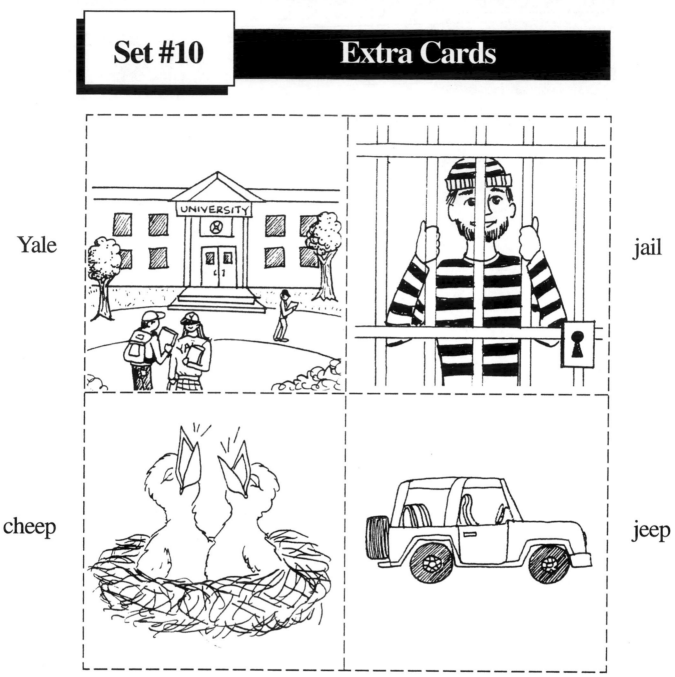

cheep

jeep

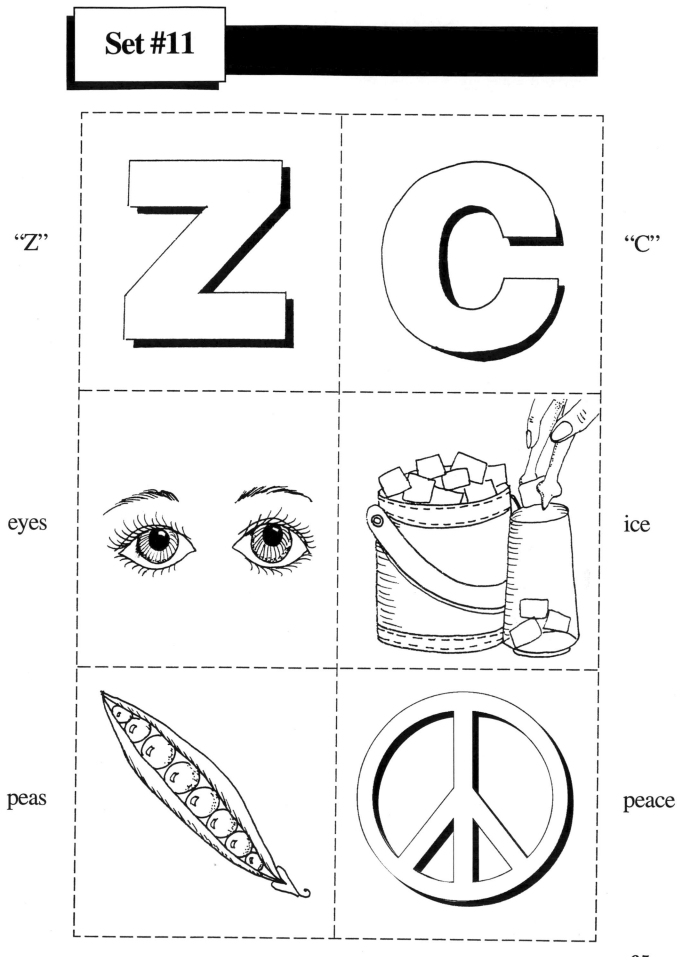

"Z"

"C"

eyes

ice

peas

peace

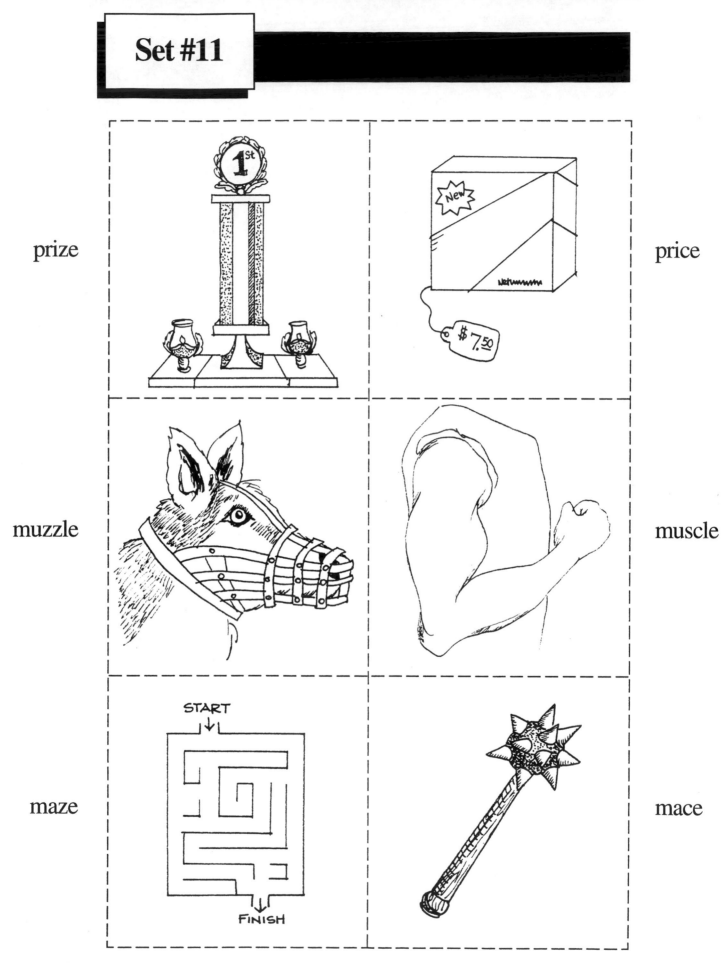

prize

price

muzzle

muscle

maze

mace

razor

racer

zinc

sink

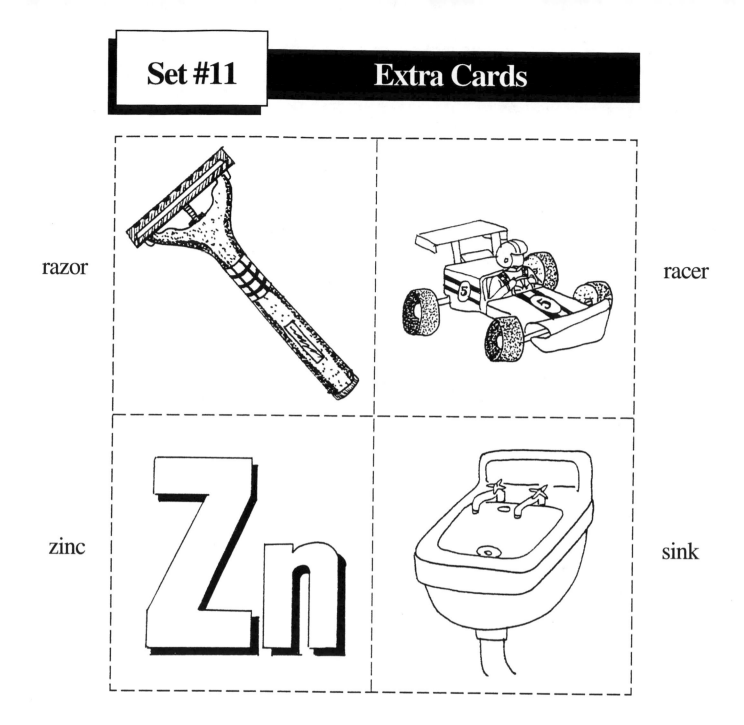

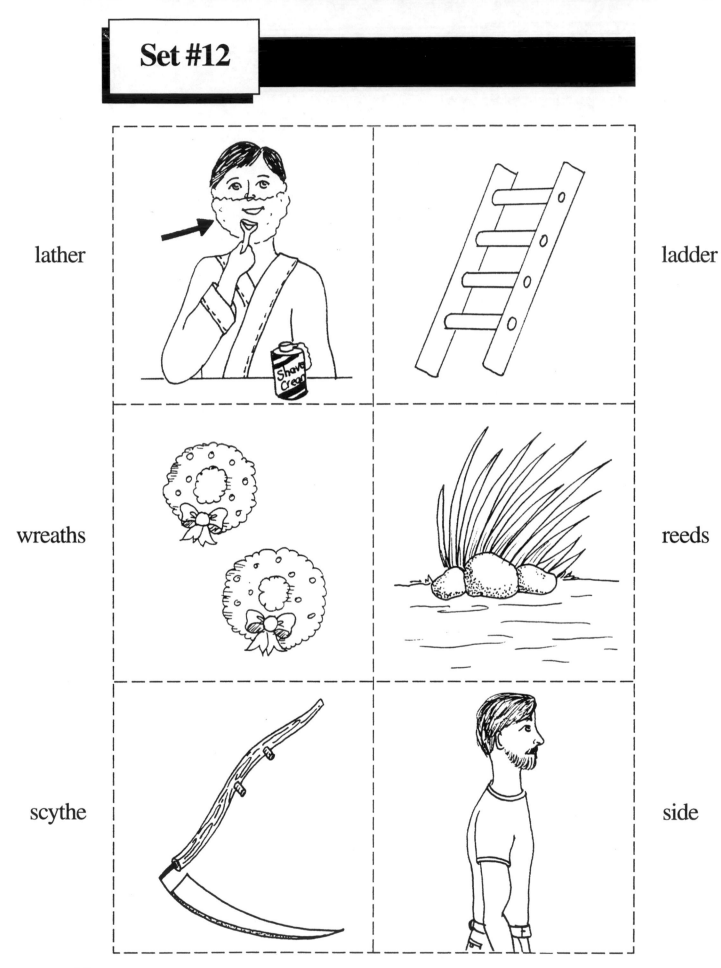

lather

ladder

wreaths

reeds

scythe

side

Set #12

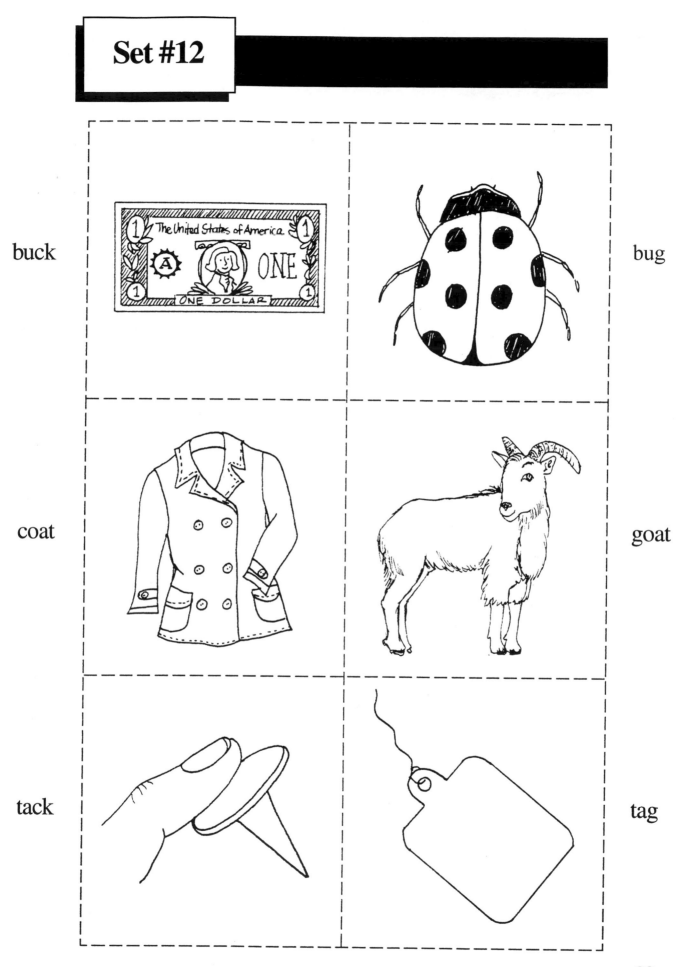

buck

bug

coat

goat

tack

tag

crane

grain

leather

letter

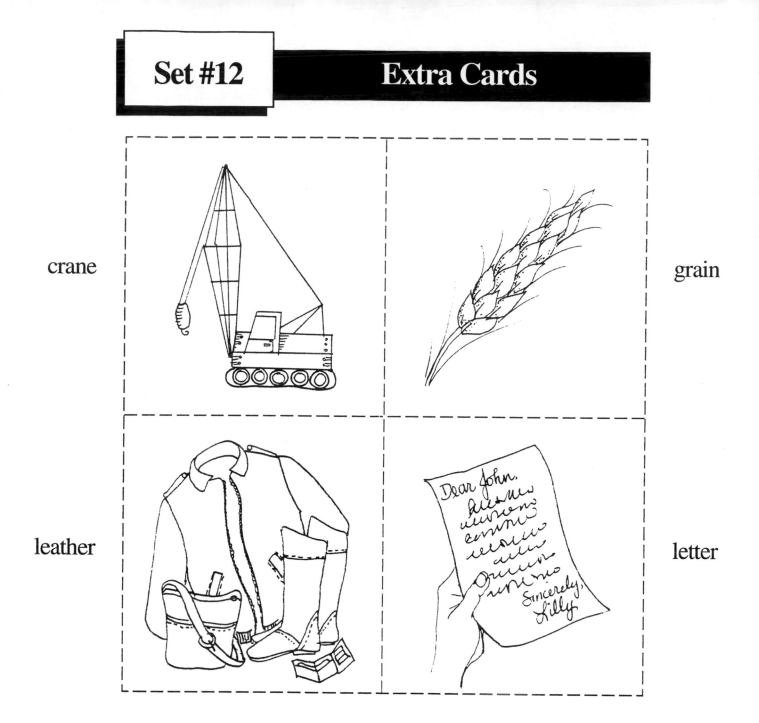

Hearts

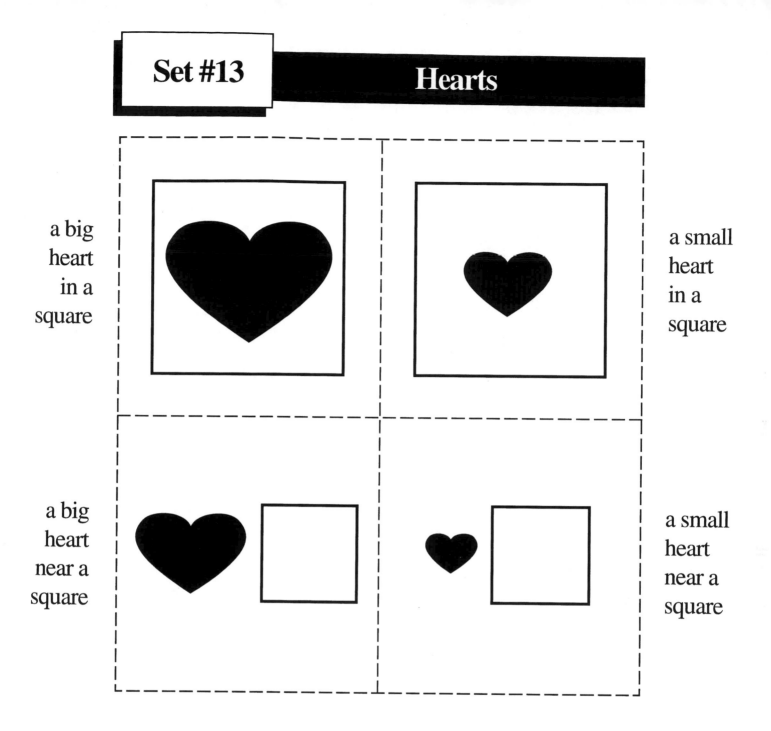

a big
heart
in a
square

a small
heart
in a
square

a big
heart
near a
square

a small
heart
near a
square

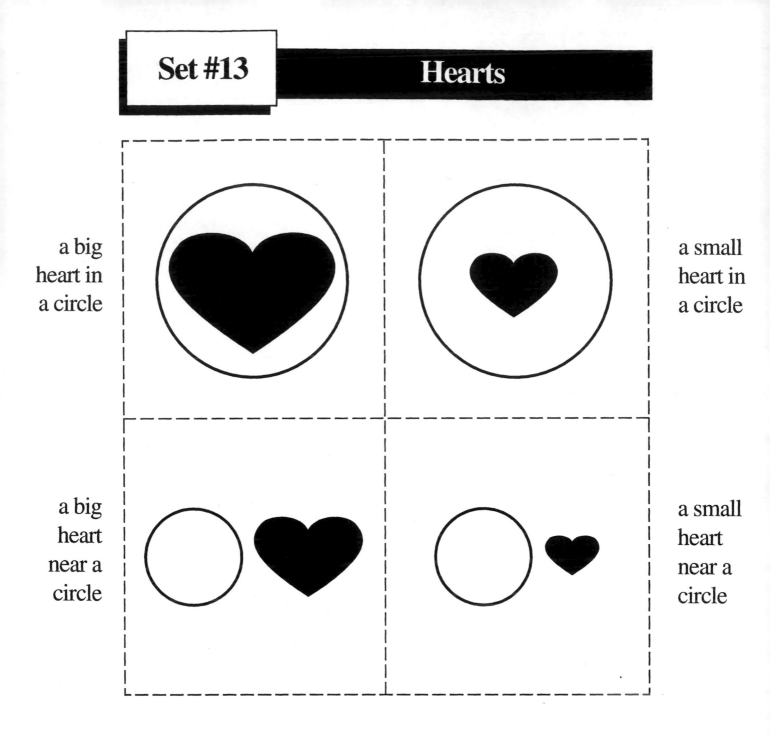

a big
heart in
a circle

a small
heart in
a circle

a big
heart
near a
circle

a small
heart
near a
circle

States & Provinces

2 Syllables	3 Syllables	4 Syllables

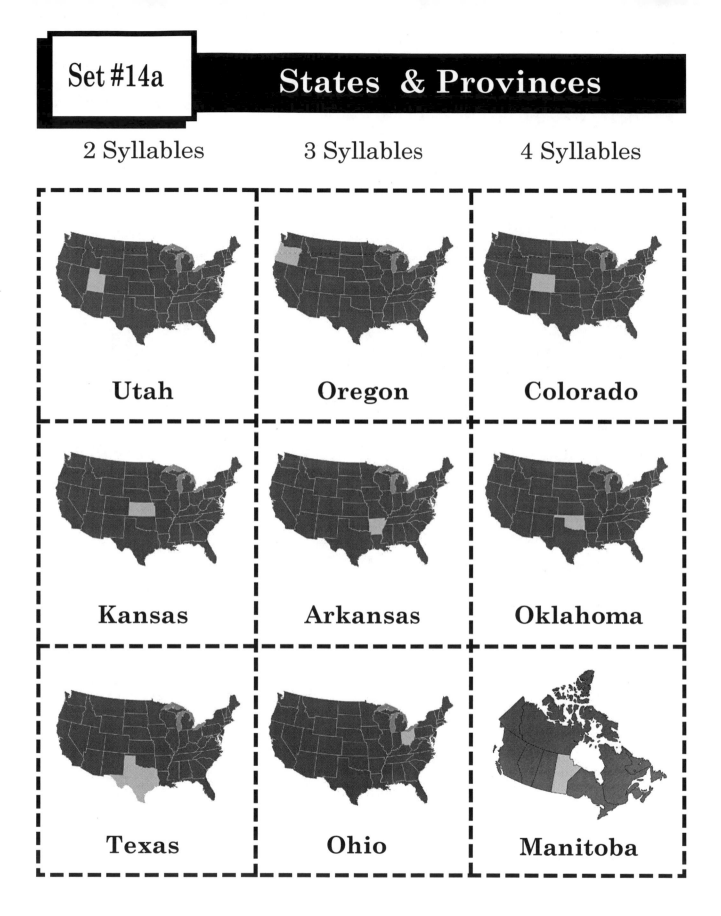

Utah	Oregon	Colorado
Kansas	Arkansas	Oklahoma
Texas	Ohio	Manitoba

States & Provinces

2 Syllables **3 Syllables** **4 Syllables**

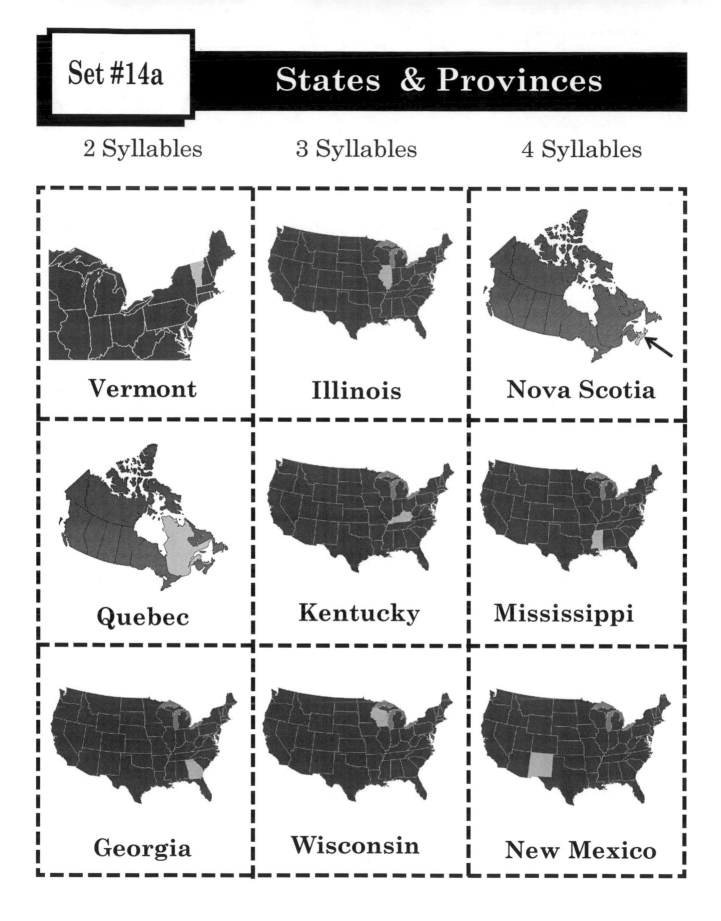

Vermont	Illinois	Nova Scotia
Quebec	Kentucky	Mississippi
Georgia	Wisconsin	New Mexico

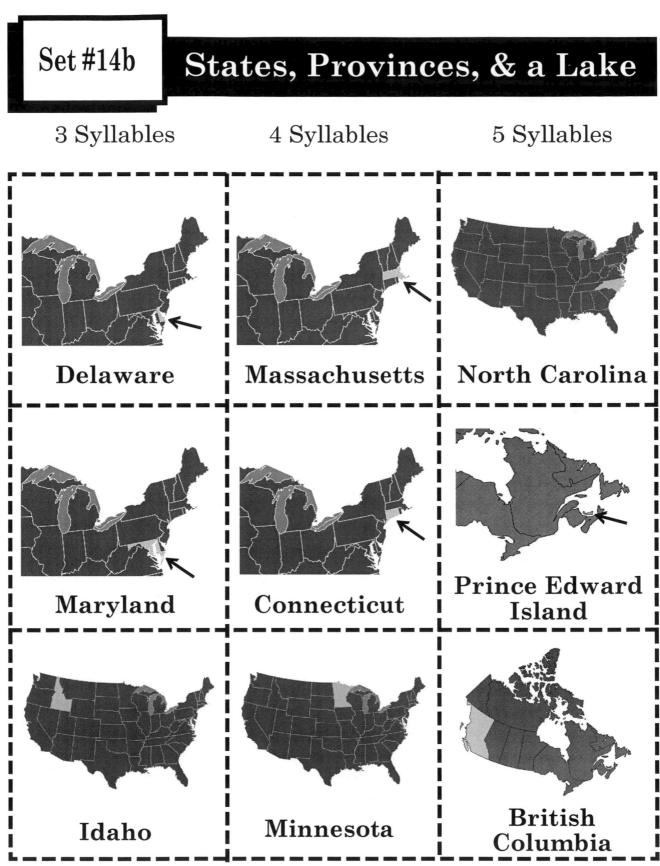

3 Syllables	4 Syllables	5 Syllables
Delaware	Massachusetts	North Carolina
Maryland	Connecticut	Prince Edward Island
Idaho	Minnesota	British Columbia

Note: Many native speakers pronounce British Columbia with 6 syllables, stressing "bi" and "a." The ends of Pennsylvania, California, and Virginia (place names given in Appendix D) follow the same pattern. The placement of these names in columns showing the number of syllables is somewhat arbitrary. However, few native speakers would hear Georgia as 3 syllables or Nova Scotia as 5.

States, Provinces, & a Lake

| 3 Syllables | 4 Syllables | 5 Syllables |

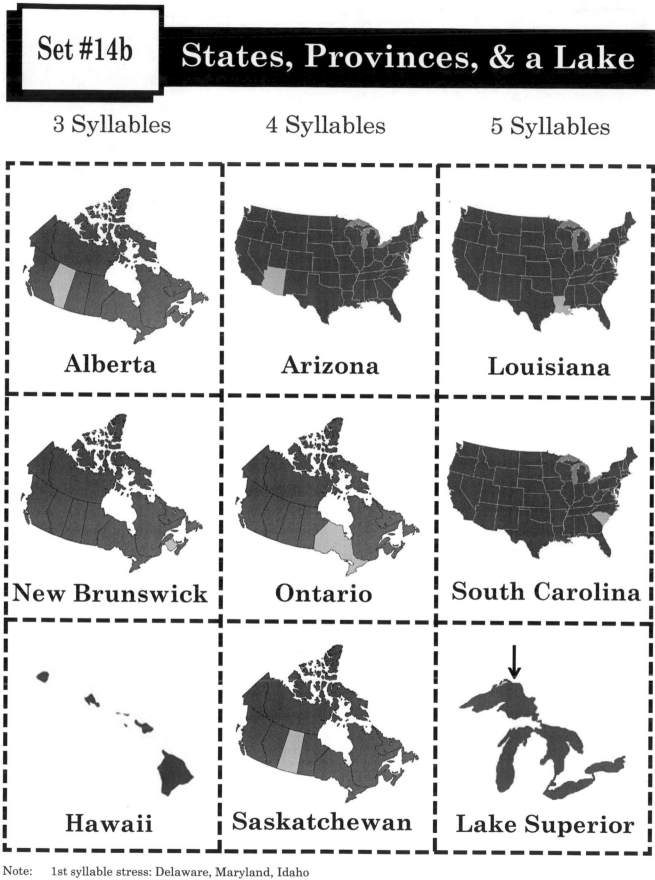

Alberta	Arizona	Louisiana
New Brunswick	Ontario	South Carolina
Hawaii	Saskatchewan	Lake Superior

Note: 1st syllable stress: Delaware, Maryland, Idaho
2nd syllable stress: Hawaii, Alberta, New Brunswick, Connecticut, Saskatchewan, Ontario
3rd syllable stress: Massachusetts, Minnesota, Arizona, Lake Superior
4th syllable stress: Prince Edward Island, South Carolina, Louisiana, North Carolina, British Columbia
See Appendix D for additional names.

Presidents

Presidents

Stress Patterns

1 George Washington

52   /   ▌ \ –

3 Thomas Jefferson

55   / –   ▌ – –

35 John F. Kennedy

56   /   /   ▌ – –

Presidents

Presidents

Stress Patterns

16 Abraham Lincoln

50 /—\   ▮ —

39 Jimmy Carter

54 /\   ▮ —

40 Ronald Reagan

58 / —   ▮ —

Presidents

Presidents	Stress Patterns

41 George Bush

53   /   ▮

36 Lyndon Baines Johnson

51   / –   / –   ▮ –

42 Bill Clinton

57   /   ▮ –

More Presidents

Presidents	Stress Patterns

2 John Adams

65   / /–

38 Gerald Ford

64   / – /

33 Harry S Truman

66   / \ / /–

More Presidents

Presidents	Stress Patterns

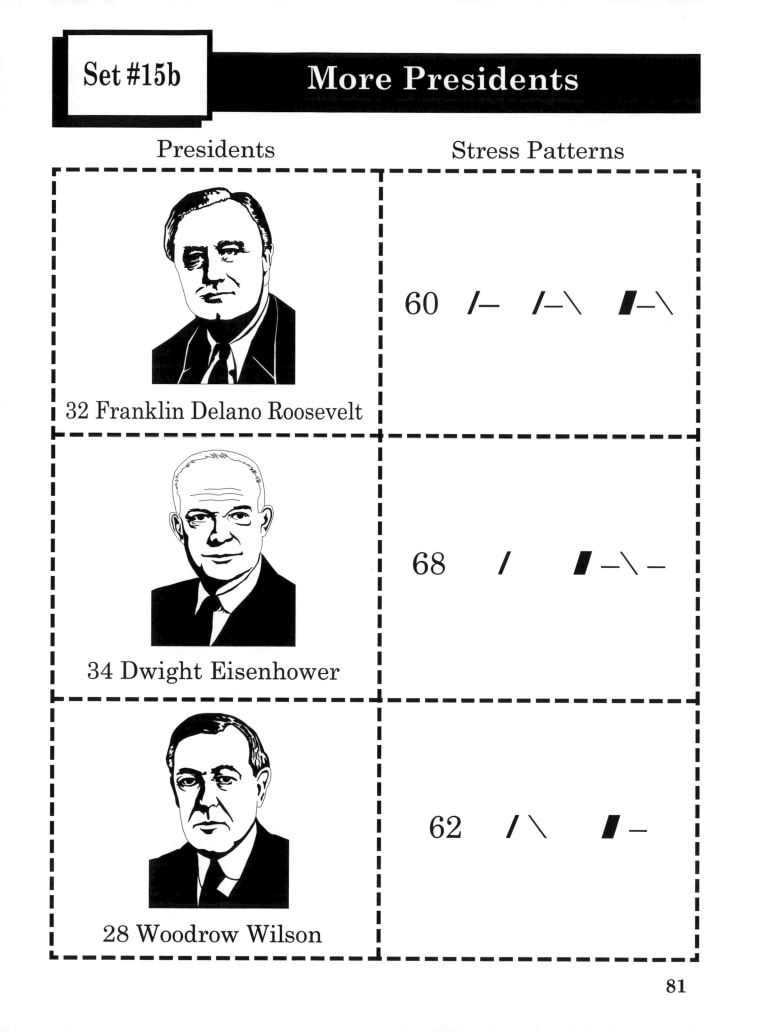

32 Franklin Delano Roosevelt

60 /— /—\ ▌—\

34 Dwight Eisenhower

68 / ▌—\—

28 Woodrow Wilson

62 /\ ▌—

More Presidents

Presidents | Stress Patterns

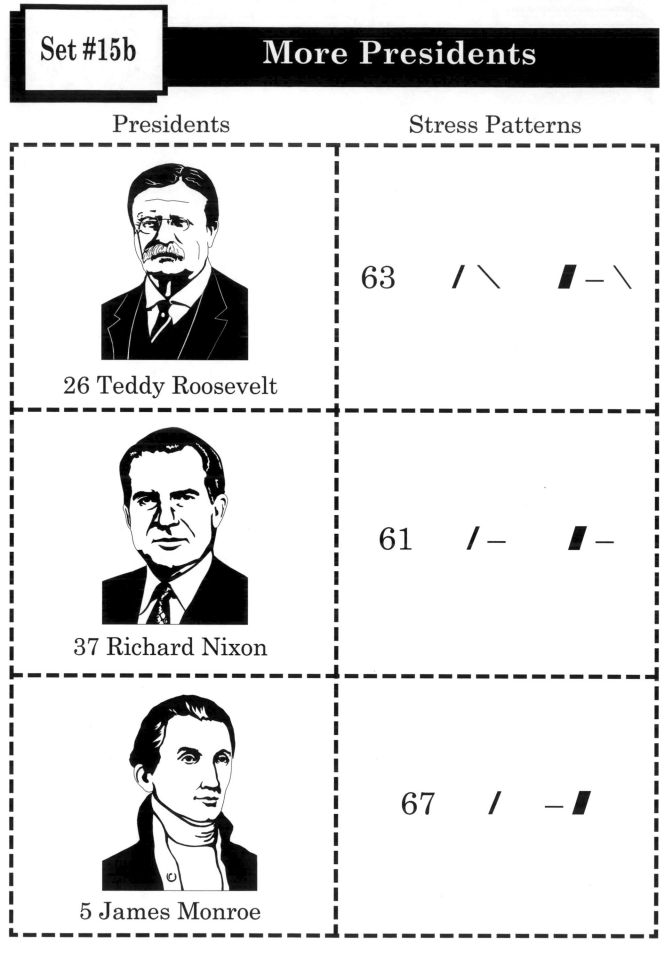

26 Teddy Roosevelt

63   / \   ▌ – \

37 Richard Nixon

61   / –   ▌ –

5 James Monroe

67   /   – ▌

Oliver Onion

Aunt Abigail

Polly Pigtails

the Bruise Brothers

drive a car

ride a bicycle

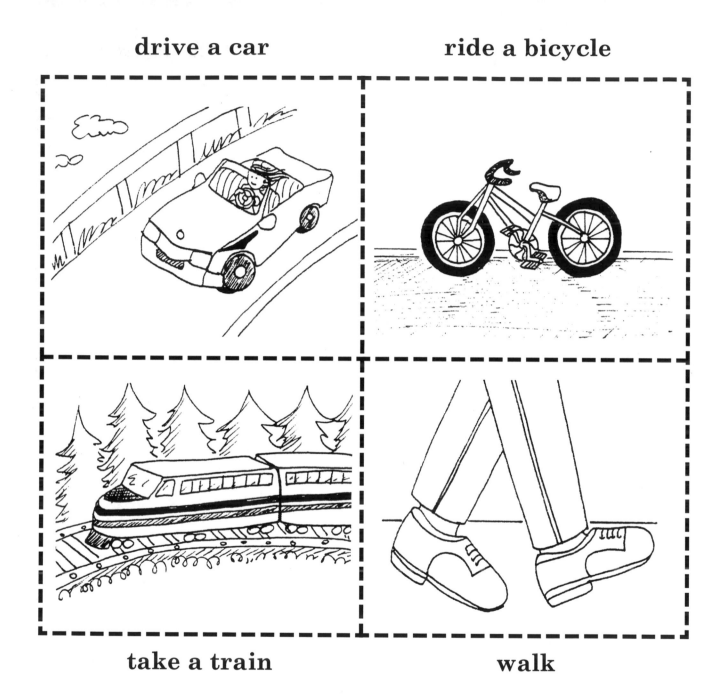

take a train

walk

home   **to the office**

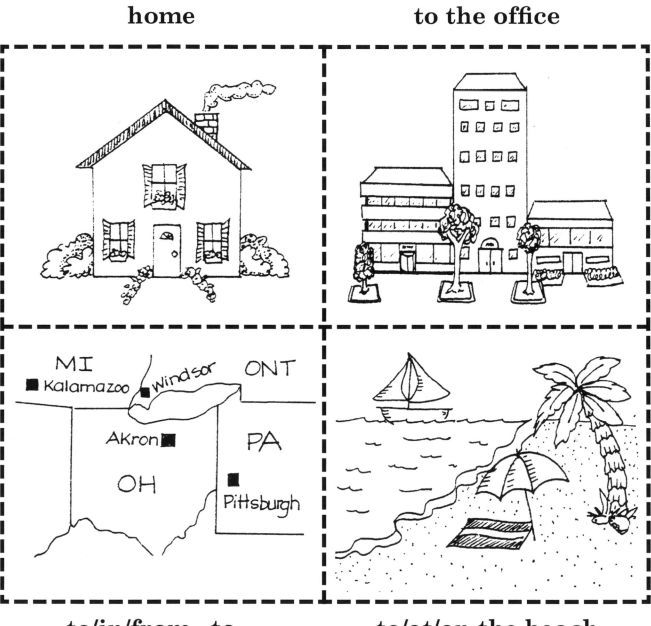

to/in/from...to...   **to/at/on the beach**

all week, this week(end), every day

today/yesterday/ tomorrow

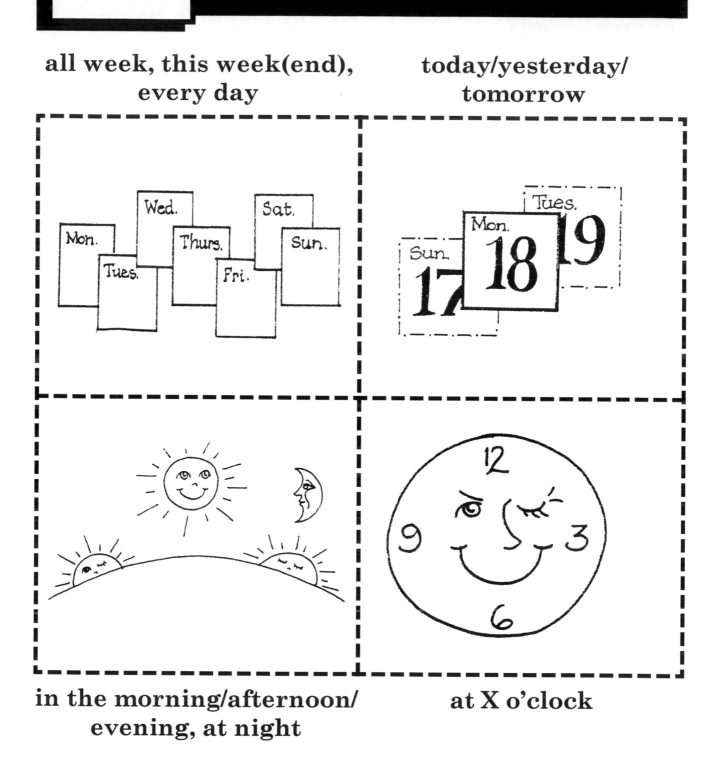

in the morning/afternoon/ evening, at night

at X o'clock

More Pro Lingua books
on pronunciation and conversation

Superphonic Bingo: Breaking the Sounds Barrier;
Fun with Phonics for Spelling and Literacy

by Maryanne Phillips Koehring. 15 photocopyable games, each with 8 differennt cards. Each game has a "teacher list" of the 55 words distributed randomly on the cards. Games progress in difficulty. Game 1 uses 5 short vowels and 9 consonants, and game 15 uses all the vowels and consonants with words beginning with Qu, Z, J, W, and Y.

From Sound to Sentence: Learning to Read and Write English;
Basic Literacy and Spelling, Phonics and Sight Words

by Raymond C. Clark. The sounds of English and their various spellings are introduced in groups throughout 14 units. Also introduced are high frequency sight words with irregular spellings, such as one, two, and eight; numbers; and cursive scripts. 3 CD's provide modeling and listening/pronunciation practice.

Pronunciation Activities: Vowels in Limericks from Adam to Ursula

by Arlene Egelberg. This is an integrated skills student text for advanced beginners to low intermediate-level students, although more advanced students will also find it useful for polishing their pronunciation. The 16 units focus on the sounds and spellings of the 16 vowel sounds of English. Students also practice consonant sounds, stress, reduction, linking, and intonation. They work on the individual sounds (*segmentals*) and the rhythm, phrasing, stress, and melody (*suprasegmentals*) of ordinary English speech. The activities in each unit are varied and fun. ***CD.***

Conversation Inspirations: Over 2400 Conversation Topics

by Nancy Zelman. A teacher resource with 8 different conversation class activities: talks, interviews, role plays, chain stories and other group activities, and discussions. Procedures for each are clearly laid out. These include topic cards, monitoring, and correction techniques, and a variety of game rituals that make the conversation class effective and enjoyable. Inexpensive, quick, and easy to use; ***photocopyable.***

Conversation Strategies: Pair and Group Activities for Developing Communicative Competence by David Kehe and Peggy Dustin Kehe.
This is an integrated skills student text for intermediate-level students, although it works well with more advanced students who don't know the strategies. There are 29 activities giving practice with the words, phrases, and conventions used to maintain effective control of conversations. Strategies include polite forms, correction, agreement and disagreement, summarization, clarifications, follow-up questions, interruptions, and avoiding conversation killers.

Stress Rulz! Rap Music Pronunciation Activities for the ESL Classroom by Janelle Fischler and Kate Jensen, performed by their students. A CD with photocopyable teacher's manual. Students learn the rules of stress in American English by listening to rap music and lyrics which explain and demonstrate the rules. The book provides the lyrics, suggestions and explanations for the teacher, as well as copyable materials for flashcards and extended activities.

Go Fish: Seven Speaking and Listening Games for Language Learning by Shawn Halwas. Practice with low-level communication, pronunciation, and vocabulary building skills – in any language. A collection of 86 pairs of brightly colored cards showing pictures of things you would find in a home, from knife, fork, and spoon to wastebasket, desk, and computer. The cards are printed on glossy paper, bound into a teacher's book, two to a page, to be cut out, laminated (optional) and used as flash cards and for playing Go Fish, Match It, Bingo, etc.

Index Card Games for ESL, edited by Raymond C. Clark. 7 game techniques for developing vocabulary, sentence/paragraph structure, pronunciation and spelling, questioning, and conversation skills through student-centered conversation activities. A "starter kit" of sample games at the elementary, intermediate, and advanced levels is given after each explanation. *Also available in French and Spanish.* **Photocopyable.**

Play 'n Talk: Communicative Games for Elementary and Middle School ESL/EFL by Gordana Petricic. 61 games to help children build conversation fluency and vocabulary, grammar, and writing skills. *45 photocopyable masters.*

Do As I Say: 55 Natural and Logical Sequences for Language Acquisition by Gayle Nelson, Thomas Winters, and Raymond C. Clark. Often humorous classroom activities in which beginning to low-intermediate students working in pairs communicate naturally and accurately to accomplish set tasks step by step.

Story Cards: North American Indian Tales, compiled by Susannah J. Clark and illustrated in color by Ken Rainbow Cougar Edwards. Students choose one of the 48 illustrated Story Cards, read the story, and then tell it from memory to a partner or to the class. Each story can be the basis for fascinating intercultural discussions.

Story Cards: Aesop's Fables, compiled by Raymond C. Clark, illustrated in color by Hannah Bonner. 48 of Aesop's wonderful, classic stories, some well-known and others not so familiar, can be used as the basis for many different conversation activities.

All of the above resources for developing pronunciation and conversation skills are available from **Pro Lingua Associates.**

www.ProLinguaAssociates.com

P.O. Box 1348, Brattleboro, Vermont 05302 USA • 800 366 4775